TAKING ON SAINTHOOD

ROBERT KRUSE

Copyright © 2021
Robert Kruse
TAKING ON SAINTHOOD
All rights reserved.

No part of this publication may be reproduced, distributed, or transmitted in any form or by any means, including photocopying, recording, or other electronic or mechanical methods, without the prior written permission of the publisher, except in the case of brief quotations embodied in critical reviews and certain other non-commercial uses permitted by copyright law.

Robert Kruse

Printed in the United States of America
First Printing 2021
First Edition 2021

ISBN: 978-0-578-93880-6

10 9 8 7 6 5 4 3 2 1

TAKING ON SAINTHOOD

Table of Contents

Introduction 1

Chapter One 3
As A Child

Chapter Two 13
Who God Is

Chapter Three 31
Who Am I?

Chapter Four 43
Relationship or Religion

Chapter Five 53
Sainthood

Chapter Six 61
Answering the Call

Chapter Seven 69
For His Glory

Chapter Eight 77
Taking Ownership

Chapter Nine 87
Caring For The Lost

Chapter Ten 93
Having the Mind of Christ

Chapter Eleven 101

Intentional

Chapter Twelve 109

Living Prophetic

Chapter Thirteen 117

Relevance

Chapter Fourteen 123

In Jesus Name

Chapter Fifteen 131

God Pleaser

Chapter Sixteen 137

Thy Kingdom Come

Chapter Seventeen 145

Perfect 10

Chapter Eighteen 157

Living in the Now

Chapter Nineteen 165

Can You See Me Now?

Chapter Twenty 173

You Are Worthy Of It All

Chapter Twenty One 181

Stand Guard

INTRODUCTION

In the 46 years that I have spent walking with Jesus a current word from scripture has always burned in my heart. The rhema of God, the spoken word, the Bible verse that shouts for application is why I study scripture. Knowing that the word is inspired by God for teaching, reproof, correction and training in righteousness not only encourages me to know it but inspires me to show it. Taking on Sainthood was written for the purpose of discipleship. Teaching the church the power of God's word that separates soul from spirit, joint (the mechanics of life) from marrow (the essence of life) and judges the thoughts and intentions of the heart. The simplicity of the gospel will always rule over the intricacies of life and walking in the Spirit of God allows us to keep an eternal perspective in a temporal world, making spiritual sense out of temporal circumstances.

Taking on Sainthood reminds the believer that they have the power to become and that who we were in the world is no longer who we are in Christ. Trials become testimonies when we lose our history in His story and embrace the position of saint, acknowledging sin but no longer being labeled by it and practicing righteousness as taught in scripture. When we allow God's word to define who we are everything changes. Our thoughts flow through the mind of Christ, our words echo the principles of God's word and our actions reflect our love for Jesus. God's word commands the church to seek after holiness and not be afraid of its calling to be like Jesus in a lost world. Too often we are distracted by our feelings and not fortified in faith, knowing that our pursuit of excellence is a worthy and achievable call in the life of a believer. 2 Peter 1:3 tells us, "seeing that His divine power has granted to us everything pertaining to life and godliness, through the true knowledge of Him who called us by His own glory and excellence."

If you want to weaken your resolve, keep labeling yourself as a sinner. Jesus suffered and died on Calvary so as to give us a holy position before the Father. We are not only sinners saved by grace but saints walking in grace; that's what being born again is all about. If you be in Christ you are a new creation, old things have passed away behold new things have come! A sinner, as described in scripture, practices sin; a saint practices righteousness. Practice is the key to truly define your position before God. Are we perfect and without sin? By no means, but our pursuit of holiness should never be overtaken by our human nature, neither should we excuse our sin based on who we were. Lenience precedes license and an excuse is the skin of reason covering a lie. Taking on Sainthood challenges us to be all that God has called us to be and not to be ignorant of our sinful nature, nor should we be ignorant of the powerful work of the Holy Spirit in becoming children of God.

Chapter One

As A Child

In John 1:12 the gospel says that to as many as received Jesus, to them He gave the power to become children of God. Throughout history no one is born a man but a child and it is that child that grows to become a sinner in need of a Savior. So it is with our spirits that are born free through our acceptance of Jesus into our lives as Savior and Lord. A Christian must first be a child at heart embracing the simplicity and purity of the gospel having a childlike faith believing that God will always be there to meet their needs according to His riches in glory. A loving Father whose only concern is for us to experience a peace that surpasses understanding and a joy that is not bound by our emotions but instead steadfast, focused on the truth that we are loved and everything will work out for the good because we love God with a childlike faith knowing that His call is our purpose.

#697 "Our treasure develops our value system forming our choices."

Being that the greatest position in the kingdom of God is child of God, pursue your sonship and you will attain your sainthood. In the natural we want to leave childish behavior behind and so we should. Taking on sainthood is taking on the responsibility to no longer think, speak or reason like a child of sin but instead allow the new child of God's love, mercy and grace to become the foundation of your Christianity. Our holiness is birthed in our born-again experience with God and this spiritual child will establish who we become throughout our lives. Every position in life we hold should be an overflow of us becoming children of God. This should be our focus and foundation with Christ being our cornerstone, the center of our attention. The natural child should no longer dictate our thinking, speaking or reasoning. We are a new creation in Christ Jesus, old things have passed away behold new things have come. Romans 8:14 says, "For all who are being led by the Spirit of God, these are sons of God."

#301 *"Always let the word of God define who you are."*

We as God's children have an obligation to the Spirit of God in obedience to His word to live calculated determined lives. The essence of truth should always overrule the mechanics of circumstances. At no time should our natural child be the center of our attention. Romans 8:16 says, "The Spirit Himself testifies with our spirit that we are children of God." The power to become will enable us to pursue God by faith and not judge God's purpose and plan based on our feelings and circumstantial evidence. We must realize that becoming will take place, the question is which child will produce the overflow-the child of sin or the child of grace? The child of sin wants to be happy at all costs; the child of grace chooses to rejoice always, pray without ceasing and in everything give thanks for that is God's will concerning us. (I Thessalonians 5:16-18)

#1071 *"When there is no joy in your day to day you become weakened by your circumstances, controlled by your feelings and susceptible to the lies of the enemy."*

Remember: Our soul is stirred by happenings and if feeling good is not an option, anxiety will be its go to response. But the spirit child enjoys the presence of God no matter what is happening. We will live soul driven or spirit led - the choice will always be ours to make. In Christ we have been given the freedom and power to choose God's eternal perspective or man's temporal limitations. A soul driven life is consumed by trials, circumstances, difficulty and abusive concerns. While life may present challenges, those challenges should never lead us away from faith and the joy of the Lord which will always be our foundational strength. On the contrary, these trials according to James provide for our spirit child growth spurts developing endurance and perfection. If we truly choose not to lead with joy and believe that Jesus is not in control when things seem out of control, we will weaken our resolve to worship with thanksgiving. Instead of the Spirit of God impacting our soul, the spirit of fear will deceive us into thinking God does not care, when in reality, God's plan is hidden in our faith. If we can withstand the temptation to judge God, we will reap the fruit of a Spirit led life in Christ. Romans 8:28 says, "And we know that God causes all things to work together for good to those who love God, and are called according to His purpose.

The soul tends to be self-centered and needs to be discipled with the truth of God's word. When we can harness our soul to worship, our emotional outbursts will be hallelujahs and not anger, praise and not pity, love and not lust, contentment and not contention, worship and not worry. Our testing will turn into testimonies of God's faithfulness and opportunities to continue the journey of becoming a child of God.

#769 "Joy is a faith driven choice that we make in order to control our natural emotional make up."

Hebrews 10:39 says, "But we are not of those who shrink back to destruction, but of those who have faith to the preserving of the soul." The key to preserving our souls lies in the spirit child that knows only one thing and that is holiness. When we prepare our hearts and minds to pre-serve Jesus in our day to day through prayer, praise and the study of God's word, we enable the spirit child the freedom to be a child of God in a world corroded by sin. Our souls will be taught to worship the Savior over self. Being childlike is key to sainthood. Too often the lies of the enemy deceive us into thinking that being a saint is taking on the responsibility to lead, when in truth, a saint develops the ability to respond to God's purpose and plan and in doing so, sets an example of how to follow. The apostle Paul says, "Be imitators of me, just as I also am of Christ." When we start believing that our leadership is key to growing the kingdom of God; we fall into the trap of self-worth over Christlikeness. The Holy Spirit is the only leader that the sphere of life around us needs.

#1134 "Example followship in your fellowship and you will extinguish the fiery darts of the enemy in regard to pride and prejudice."

Pride is thinking you have something that God has not given you, and prejudice is placing others in categories for the sake of their value toward you instead of your service to them. When you choose a seat of honor, you get up from sitting at the feet of Jesus and separate yourself from the power to become, thinking you have arrived, when in reality you have only become susceptible to the lies of the enemy. In Luke 14:11 Jesus says, "For everyone who exalts himself will be humbled, and he who humbles himself will be exalted."

Every position in life that we have been honored with by God will always flow from our childlike faith and should reflect love, joy and peace in the Holy Spirit. Purity will always precede power: that spiritual place in a temporal world where Jesus is on the throne, godly wisdom is in the forefront of our thoughts and grace is the purpose as to why we speak.

#1106 *"Our words should reflect the love and wisdom of God."*

Ephesians 4:29 tells us, "Let no unwholesome word proceed from your mouth, but only such a word as is good for edification according to the need of the moment, so that it will give grace to those who hear." Every thought initiates a word or action. As children of God we have been given the power to hold every thought captive in obedience to Christ. Our words should reflect our spirit life and a focus towards God. When we control our thoughts, we control our vocabulary. Paul tells us that not one word should be spoken that would produce harm to the sphere of life around us. We do not accidentally speak foul words; they are a result of foul thoughts unchecked by our spirit. Our thoughts and words teach us how important it is to prepare ourselves with grace in every moment of our eternity. Our natural tendencies are always to break down not build up. What proceeds out of our mouth through renegade thoughts are choices we make and a clear reflection of our hearts. So as we move on to sainthood, let's remember that God has given us safeguards that will help us in the becoming process.

#952 *"Every thought producing a word resulting in an action should be worship to God and a witness to others."*

The first safeguard is the power to hold every thought captive in Christ. Do not take this safeguard lightly. Thoughts are the enemies main component in his arsenal.

His schemes are centered on our mind because our mind is the gateway to our soul, the seat of our feelings, emotions and choices. If the enemy can control our thoughts, our words will soon follow leading to behavior that is unbecoming that of a child of God. Psalms 19:14 says, "Let the words of my mouth and the meditation of my heart be acceptable in Your sight, O

Lord, my rock and my Redeemer." And again in Proverbs 23:12, "Apply your heart to discipline and your ears to words of knowledge." If we as Christians can win over our hearts to love and serve Jesus, our battle against self and Satan will be won before a word is spoken. Developing the mind of Christ will enable us to proclaim words of healing and not hurt, and we will spend more time praising God and less time repenting for worthless words spoken. The choice is ours. We can choose life or death, victory or defeat, being content with holiness or satisfied with self. It all begins with one thought held captive in Christ or left unchecked.

#306 *"The mind of man is an important part of establishing the heart of God."*

The second safeguard is the power to hold or release the spoken word. In short, it is the power of the tongue. Jehoshaphat, king of Judah, speaks a rarely used Bible verse on whether or not he should partner with King Ahab of Israel in regard to going to battle against Ramoth-Gilead. 2 Chronicles 18:4 tells us, "Moreover, Jehoshaphat said to the king of Israel, 'Please inquire first for the word of the Lord'." Being deliberate in prayer for every day that the Lord has made will cause us to rejoice and be glad in it, no matter what it may present to us. (Psalms 118:24)

#1083 *"The power to become must happen before the power to overcome is necessary."*

Our prayer life is the becoming factor that allows us to apply God's written word to our spoken word. If we are being deliberate and quick to listen and slow to speak, we are inviting the power of God's word and the influence of his Holy Spirit to define who we are in the words we speak. The word 'let' in Ephesians 4:29 tells us we can control our tongue if we have prepared ourselves through prayer and Bible study. We can stop words if we choose to for the glory of God. The book of James 3:6 tells us, "And the tongue is a fire, the very world of iniquity; the tongue is set among our members as that which defiles the entire body, and sets on fire the course of our life, and is set on fire by hell." But once redeemed it shares the good news of the gospel of peace, edifying those who hear it, bringing grace to those in need, and providing comfort to the downtrodden, sharing the love of Jesus to the lost world ensnared by the corruption of sin. Our words should make a difference for the sake of the kingdom. Once we spoke darkness and pain, but now we have been given the power to speak the truth of God's word in light and love. This safeguard allows us to make spiritual sense in the temporal world, bound by the limitations of circumstances and enthralled by emotional reaction instead of spiritual response. Ephesians 4:15 says, "But speaking the truth in love, we are to grow up in all aspects into Him who is the head, even Christ." How we speak reflects our belief system and our words expose our hearts. When we determine in our hearts to know nothing except Jesus Christ and Him crucified, we will speak nothing but words that build up and encourage life in the Spirit and a focus towards God.

#261 *"Teach eternity in every temporal circumstance."*

Our tongue will easily relapse if we try to live on yesterday's victories. Today is the day of salvation and with every new day comes the opportunity to not only grow in Jesus but to witness to others the power of God's love through our words. We should not only pray the word of God, but speak the word of God. Maybe not by chapter and verse, but by principal and truth. The prophet Micaiah in II Chronicles 18:13 says, "As the Lord lives, what my God says, that I will speak." Do not ever say I did not mean to say that. All of our words are formed deliberately by our thought patterns. Our words will define our relationship with Jesus and expose either a carnal mind or a heart for God.

The third safeguard is the power to act upon God's promises. In having the power to become, and everything pertaining to life and godliness through Jesus, our actions will always speak louder than our words. The life of Jesus established our redemption and validated His works. Faith is an action word that, without deeds, produces nothing but religious jargon. Faith that is not lived out is worthless to the sphere of life around us. In Matthew 5:16 Jesus says, "Let your light shine before men in such a way that they may see your good works, and glorify your Father who is in heaven." Words are heard, good works are seen. If you want to live a forgetful life, tell people about Jesus without giving them a visual example of what that means.

#1035 *"Faith is having the power to move on when God's purpose proves different from our plans."*

Faith reminds us that God is alive and His presence is worth living for. Hearing, speaking and walking are all essential parts of Christlike behavior. But walking shows God and others the reality of our faith. Believing precedes obeying, obedience to God's word is in direct relationship with our faith in God's presence. Every choice that we make is a testimony of whether or not we believe that Jesus Christ rose from the dead and will never leave us or forsake us. Faith without works is worthless, because faith unseen is not faith at all, just a religious thought that may tickle the ear but not bring healing to the heart. God did not think about sending His Son to die for our sins, He did. Jesus did not think about going to the cross and sacrificing His life for the forgiveness of our sins, He did. If we want to live redeemed, we must act like God's love, mercy and grace really matter. Romans 13:14 says, "But put on the Lord Jesus Christ, and make no provision for the flesh in regard to its lusts."

Paul also wrote in Galatians 5:16, "But I say, walk by the Spirit, and you will not carry out the desire of the flesh."

#1112 *"The Spirit of truth should always overrule the mechanics of circumstances".*

When we allow the soul of man to inspire our actions, feelings will control our behavior and not our faith in God and His promises. If you have to go through trials, it is better to do so with holiness of heart and mind, knowing that trials are God-given opportunities to grow in Jesus. We miss out on teachable moments from God when we react to circumstances in an emotional rather than a spiritual manner. Putting on Jesus in the morning helps keep us from putting off the Spirit filled walk that empowers us to fulfill life and godliness in our day to day and to disable the never-ending desires of our flesh.

How we act in the day is usually a clear reflection of how we prepare ourselves in the morning. A child of God should get up, get dressed and have a healthy spiritual breakfast. Jesus tells us to be dressed in readiness and keep our lamps lit. If Jesus, the light of our world, simply becomes a religious figurine that we give homage to but not our whole hearts, we will be at risk of missing the truth of God's reality and be distracted by the world, devil and the flesh. Constant Christianity is key to rejoicing always, praying without ceasing and in everything giving thanks, for this is the will of God concerning us. Our human tendencies are to compartmentalize life in different categories and in doing so, never allow the fullness of God to embrace the wholeness of man. We live differently based on where we are and who we are supposed to be, creating hypocrisy within our testimony of Jesus. We act not based on truth but circumstances, holding firm to what we believe is our responsibility for that category of life.

This kind of behavior may in itself seem somewhat noble, but from an eternal perspective, it limits God's purpose and plan. When we think we have to behave a certain way based on our categorical circumstances, we limit the basic foundation of who we are in God's eyes and perform at work, school, church and home in a way that hinders God's power to become children of God. Remember: We have been given the power to respond to Him as a child in every position granted to us from God. Sainthood is easily embraced when we realize that our actions should glorify the Father in every aspect of our life.

Different places of worship, whether it be work, school, church or family are simply opportunities to be taught and teach a childlike faith in the midst of the sphere of life around us.

#240 *"You cannot forget your spiritual position in pursuit of worldly goals."*

We will have responsibilities in every phase of our life's journey, whether we rejoice in those phases will be based on whether or not we choose to acknowledge Jesus as our foundation and build on Him. Remember: Sainthood is not growing out of childlike faith but growing into it.

Chapter Two
Who God Is

The character of God found in the fruit of the Spirit sets the goals for our day to day. Galatians 5:22-23 says, "But the fruit of the Spirit is love, joy, peace, patience, kindness, goodness, faithfulness, gentleness, self-control; against such things there is no law." These are the fruit of the Spirit, all as one and one representing all. They cannot be separated and still reflect the character of God; the fruit of the Spirit is who God is. Our flesh sets its desire against the Spirit of God, and so the Spirit against the flesh; they are in opposition to one another. For that which was pleasing to us before receiving Jesus will rise up against us as we attempt to please God in Christ. Pursuing the fruit of the Spirit creates a heart and mindset that crucifies the flesh along with its lusts in pursuit of holiness, taking full advantage of the divine power granted to us through a true knowledge of Him who called us by His own glory and excellence. Having the power to become allows the fruit of the Spirit to solidify our position as children of God, establishing our sainthood in light of God's character, a testimony of our born free lifestyle. If we have been given everything pertaining to life and godliness and the Holy Spirit is working in us by faith, then the fruit of the Spirit is waiting, available for us to pick and use for God's glory.

Let us begin with the fruit of **love**. I Corinthians 13:4-8 tells us that "Love is patient, love is kind and is not jealous; love does not brag and is not arrogant, does not act unbecomingly; it does not seek its own, is not provoked, does not take into account a wrong suffered, does not rejoice in unrighteousness, but rejoices with the truth; bears all things, believes all things, hopes all things, endures all things. Love never fails…"

If we would practice unconditional love nothing in our lives would deprive us from unconditional worship and a lifestyle reflecting a personal walk with Jesus. We could close this book and spend the rest of our lives moving from glory to glory. But life and our human make up does not seem to surrender to the mystery of God's love. We easily get entangled with circumstances that hinder love in our day to day. But that does not mean we stop pursuing righteousness, on the contrary, we will never be perfect but our goal in the process of becoming is to never give up on perfection. Sainthood depends on it. So as you study the fruit of the Spirit, do not be intimidated by its seemingly unachievable status, stay in the moment. Let God take care of your eternity.

#75 "If we aren't living eternity moment by moment, something is seriously wrong with our perspective."

In Christ we have been given the power to love with one condition, to love unconditionally. Unconditional love is who God is and everything we have been given comes from who God is. So always love with God in heart and mind, not based on what others say or do but instead on who God is. Romans 5:8 tells us, "But God demonstrates His own love toward us, in that while we were yet sinners, Christ died for us."

#722 "When we are motivated by God's love, circumstances merely provide us with opportunities to worship and witness God's faithfulness."

Unconditional love casts out fear, covers a multitude of sins, and never fails. Our spiritual freedom to choose makes love possible. And so it is with **joy**, the choice to rejoice in and through all things is made possible through our spiritual freedom to choose. Joy symbolizes trust and confidence in God being in control even when everything seems out of control. James 1:2-4 says, "Consider it all joy, my brethren, when you encounter various trials, knowing that the testing of your faith produces endurance. And let endurance have its perfect result, so that you may be perfect and complete, lacking in nothing." The word consider in the Greek means to lead with, and in doing so we prioritize joy in the midst of difficulties. Joy has nothing to do with feelings but instead the power of worship based on the promises of God found in Scripture. A godly perspective leads to joy.

#924 "Praise is a spiritual response that overrides the negative reaction of circumstances."

Discipling the soul to rejoice is a key element in spiritual warfare. When joy is heartfelt, our faith in Jesus withstands the attack of our enemies, allowing us to focus on spiritual solutions to solve our problems-not man's opinions. Joy is a mysterious fruit that lives in the now, yet sees things based on God's fulfilled purpose not so much the developmental process that it takes to get there. That is why faith plays such an important role in our rejoicing. Joy sees our present based on our future. Hebrews 12:2 tells us, "Fixing our eyes on Jesus, the author and perfecter of faith, who for the joy set before Him endured the cross, despising the shame, and has sat down at the right hand of the throne of God." If we are not living our day to day based on faithful joy, we will miss those moments of development that makes our becoming possible. The life of Jesus exemplifies the character of God. The joy set before Him was the result of our redemption, God's love, mercy and grace in exchange for our sins on Calvary. Jesus despised our sin, but loved us unconditionally. Joy separates the sin from the sinner, the trials of life from the purpose and plan of God and keeps us living in the moment with an eternal perspective seeing beyond the temporal.

#331 *"Joy is not based on the happenings in the world around you, but instead the promises of God's word within you."*

The power to overcome is most evident in joy because it reflects within our countenance a contentment that says God is in control. There are three aspects of joy:

A **calm delight**, when in the midst of trials and struggles we continue to show our trust in Jesus based on the power of praise.

Cheerfulness is another aspect of joy that is evident in our day to day where neither good times or bad times matter, only a joy reflected in our God times.

And finally **exceeding joy**, where everything is going our way and the choice to rejoice comes with less resolve and determination.

All three aspects of joy should be in play throughout the duration of our lives at one time or another. Joy is that light that shines in darkness but is also visible in our day to day. Nehemiah 8:10 says, "… for the joy of the Lord is your strength." The power to become is demonstrated in joy. Strongholds are broken when praise takes the place of pity and faith overrules circumstantial evidence. Anger is a result of feeling sorry for yourself.

#1180 *"We endure today by joyfully anticipating God's faithfulness for tomorrow."*

Our third character quality of God is **peace**. Jesus is referred to as the Prince of Peace. He spoke much of peace when He walked the earth. John 14:27 says, "Peace I leave with you; My peace I give to you; not as the world gives do I give to you. Do not let your heart be troubled, nor let it be fearful."

And again in John 16:33, "These things I have spoken to you, so that in Me you may have peace. In the world you have tribulation, but take courage; I have overcome the world." True peace is not necessarily a place of tranquility but a place of transformation. Peace is not the absence of conflict but the presence of God. This peace is not found in those who conform to this world, but those who are transformed by the renewing of their hearts and minds in Christ. This slice of the fruit of the Spirit is also established through faith and choice. Acknowledging God's presence throughout our day to day keeps peace in our hearts and empowers us to respond to the truth of God's word and not react to trials and temptations. The Bible teaches us that we have the power to keep troubling circumstances from affecting our hearts, reducing the spirit of fear into a vain attempt of the enemy to deprive us of the courage necessary to be victorious throughout our day to day. The key to peace is found in Christ: Jesus says in Me you will find peace. Gethsemane teaches us a powerful lesson, even though the soul of Jesus was troubled, He made choices for our redemption based on His spiritual relationship with the Father. Matthew 26:38-39 says, "My soul is deeply grieved, to the point of death...My Father, if it is possible, let this cup pass from Me; yet not as I will, but as You will." Knowing God's will releases us to obey God's word. Jesus acknowledged pain, but was never controlled by it. Our submission to God's will allows us to walk in the privilege of peace. Only the chosen of God in Christ can experience the peace of God in a world filled with pitfalls, stumbling blocks, delays and obstacles. Not so for the disciples in Gethsemane when Jesus was arrested and taken by the mob. Scripture says all the disciples fled. The spirit of fear played a demonic role in their behavior.

Fear challenges God's love for us, weakens our resolve towards God, and allows anxious thoughts to slip into our soul, the seat of our feelings and emotions. Jesus knew the Father loved Him, was empowered by that love and rebuked any thought neglecting God's purpose and plan for our lives.

Proverbs 19:23 says, "The fear of the Lord leads to life, so that one may sleep satisfied, untouched by evil." The spirit of fear can't even visit a child of God walking in reverence towards Jesus. Anxious thoughts should play no role in your decision-making process, only a complete trust in God's presence and faithfulness.

#46 *"Peace is living what faith in God's word proclaims."*

Finally we find Peter following from a distance. I believe giving thanks was the last thing on Peter's mind and in his heart that day in Gethsemane, yet his redemption was at play. Peter and all the disciples knew that Jesus must go to Jerusalem and suffer many things from the elders and chief priests and scribes, to be killed and raised up on the third day. (Matthew 16:21) Yet when we follow Jesus from a distance, peace is replaced with panic resulting in denial. When we distance ourselves from the truth of God's word, praying in the spirit and worshiping at all times, we fall prey to anxiety and our interests take priority over God's purpose. Denial produces denial, if you deny the truth of God's word you will deny His peace that surpasses all understanding guarding your heart and mind in the midst of God's purpose and plan.

#571 *"Pilgrims progress...For every problem God gives a promise linked to a principal leading to a provision and as we persevere through the process God will accomplish His purpose so be at peace."*

II Peter 1:2-3 says, "Grace and peace be multiplied to you in the knowledge of God and of Jesus our Lord; seeing that His divine power has granted to us everything pertaining to life and godliness, through the true knowledge of Him who called us by His own glory and excellence." We have the power to live in peace if we truly believe that the Prince of Peace is true to His word and that He is alive and living in us. He will keep you in perfect peace if you keep your mind stayed on Him. (Isaiah 26:3) If God's divine power has granted to us everything needed to walk in the Spirit and to keep our focus towards God, then peace will replace anxiety as our minds remain steadfast only releasing that which embodies our knowledge of God and not the schemes of the devil. Perfect peace is not wishful thinking but practical living.

Are you patient? **Patience** is that character quality of God that acts as a continuance factor in the fruit of the Spirit. Patience allows love, joy, peace, kindness, goodness, faithfulness, gentleness and self-control to continue and never stops reflecting the quality of life found in Christ.

#27 *"Impatience does not trust the Father or His timing."*

Impatience excuses, justifies, and compromises our faith in God's presence. Patience will always reflect trust in the midst of trials and never gives God a deadline in regard to answered prayer. Patience is that slice of fruit that determines to trust in the Lord with all of our heart and does not lean on our own understanding, in all of our ways acknowledge Him, knowing that in His time He will straighten out our paths in life. Our lack of patience limits God's power and allows the enemy to deceive us, convincing us that God does not care or worse does not love us. And just as the serpent deceived Eve in his craftiness, we too would be led astray from the simplicity and purity of the gospel that calls us to wait on the Lord and not be distracted by what we do not understand. Patience is a mysterious fruit in which nothing is done but the character of God is revealed. Our human tendencies are to take control of our circumstances. Patience releases control and focuses on God's will be done. It exposes hope to the lost world, that joyful anticipation that in spite of what is seen, believes in what is true allowing the truth of God's word to grow and produce.

#898 *"Hope confesses a lack of understanding, and is not afraid of the unknown."*

Patience dissolves the influence against our soul to excuse bad language and behavior based on people and circumstances. Instead it disciples the soul in regard to the faithfulness of God, knowing that Jesus will never leave us or forsake us and if we place our trust in Him, He will never disappoint us.

Patience never gets tired of holding every thought captive in obedience to Christ, going the second mile, being anxious for nothing, standing on the promises, rejoicing always, praying without ceasing and in everything giving thanks, turning law into liberty and duty into privilege. When we are yoked with Jesus our day to day will reflect an intentional cadence with His Spirit, leaving no room for doubt, only a testimony of God's faithfulness. Patience keeps us from falling behind or moving ahead of God's Spiritual cadence. It is that cadence that keeps our flesh from creating doubt and circumstances from controlling our feelings. Patience is that eternal influence that never says never or is swayed by what seems to be, but instead, of what God's word proclaims and promises.

#1040 *"A temporal perspective limits God's eternal plan."*

The enemies of our souls; the world, the flesh and the devil, want nothing more than for us to focus fully on the here and now with little thought in regard to eternity. Our God is an eternal being always been and never ending. Eternity is God's timetable and Jesus is the setpoint in which we begin our journey of life in the Spirit. From the moment we receive Jesus we enter into eternal life. Everyone must take the path of Jesus to find freedom from a temporal world calling us to feast on its pleasures, be wise in its sin, and deceived by its prince. Jesus truly is the way, truth and life; no one will experience eternity with the Father but through Him.

(John 14:6) Our greatest example of patience is found in God's love, mercy and grace. His eternal plan for redemption is based on patience. Our Father has set aside a time when justice will be served and His final call will come to a lost world and only the Father knows when that last day will be. The trumpet will sound and His love, mercy and grace will be fulfilled. Faith will no longer be necessary, we will see Him in the fullness of His glory, no pain, no shame, no regrets, only joy unexplainable, unspeakable and unimaginable. But until that day our anticipation is to fulfill His likeness to the best of our ability in our lives. Patiently loving unconditionally, not giving others what they deserve and blessing the sphere of life around us with what they do not deserve: mercy and grace. If we can keep before us God's love, mercy and grace and embrace it with gratitude living with fortitude, patience will not be a struggle but a testimony of God's power displayed in the fruit of the Spirit. His character will be obvious and the silence of patience will shout hallelujah in our day to day.

#777 "Unconditional trust releases unconditional love in our day to day."

Are you kind? **Kindness** is that slice of God's character that reflects grace in a lost world. Unmerited favor should be intentional, based on God's love not people's behavior. When we determine to know nothing except Jesus Christ and Him crucified to the glory of God and the salvation of man, will we introduce kindness to the sphere of life around us. The mysteries of God in Christ have been made known to us based on His kind intentions, not our performance. When we deprive others of God's kindness, we restrict them from God's will and satisfy our own wants instead. II Corinthians 12:9 says, "...My grace is sufficient for you, for power is perfected in weakness. Most gladly, therefore, I will rather boast about my weaknesses, so that the power of Christ may dwell in me." Our soul is once again confronted with power and how it should be displayed in our day to day.

Our human tendencies are more inclined to be abrupt and authoritative instead of kind. Power without kindness is bullying.

#57 *"Kindness is a godly temperament that delights in contributing to the welfare of others."*

If we see life through kind eyes, others will benefit from God's grace empowering them to become all that He has called them to be. Our kind intentions towards others will release God's love, mercy and grace establishing an environment of spiritual growth, not condemnation. But before we can minister to others, we must first accept and understand that God's kindness towards us is true no matter what the circumstances may bring. Only when that reality has been established in our lives will kindness be a lifestyle seen and received by others. God's grace is demonstrated through His kindness. Ephesians 2:7-8 says, "So that in the ages to come He might show the surpassing riches of His grace in kindness toward us in Christ Jesus. For by grace you have been saved through faith; and that not of yourselves, it is the gift of God." There is nothing in ourselves that can produce godly kindness. When we take on sainthood, we take on spiritual authority, not worldly position. Our salvation is based on God's kindness towards us. Kindness sees beyond the faults of man and touches their needs in Christ. The kindness of God was represented to us in Jesus, when we receive Him we receive the power to be kind. Titus 3:4-5 says, "But when the kindness of God our Savior and His love for mankind appeared, He saved us, not on the basis of deeds which we have done in righteousness, but according to His mercy, by the washing of regeneration and renewing by the Holy Spirit." Jesus is the embodiment of kindness. When we are kind, we are saying to the sphere of life around us that Jesus is alive in us.

#1117 *"The overflow of our relationship with Jesus is kindness to the sphere of life around us."*

The next slice of the fruit of the Spirit is **goodness**. This fruit has been misinterpreted more than any fruit of the Spirit by the world to justify favor from God based on being a good person and not needing God's plan of redemption and the need for repentance from its sins. The world would separate sin into categories, making lesser sins self-redeemed based on good works, finding no need for the cross of Calvary and the life, death and resurrection of Jesus unnecessary for the forgiveness of sin. The fruit of the Spirit goodness is woven into the character of God and cannot be separated from God's holiness. Good minus God equals "o". Worldly goodness cannot provide salvation leading to eternal blessings, but instead a false security leading to bondage in this age and in the age to come, eternal death. Goodness originates from God and can only be obtained through faith in Christ Jesus. God's grace empowers us in accomplishing good works, not our natural ability. We in ourselves are inherently rebellious, but in Christ we exchange our rebellion for righteous living. II Corinthians 9:8 says, "And God is able to make all grace abound to you, so that having all sufficiency in everything, you may have abundance for every good deed."

When we take on sainthood it is important to understand that we have all sufficiency in all things, at all times, to do good in a lost world. Goodness is a spiritual choice that reflects God's character no matter what the circumstances may be. To be filled with the Spirit is to be filled with goodness that leads others to glorify the Father through a personal relationship with Jesus. (Matthew 5:16) Be sure to take no credit in your goodness towards others and it will be credited to you as a child of God through the power of the Spirit of God. Humility plays an important part of God's goodness; it keeps us on the straight and narrow.

#508 *"Greatness serves with honor yet walks with humility."*

A humble heart never views accomplishments as achievements only success in fulfilling God's purpose. Success in this world is seen as highpoints in life, but our day to day walk with Jesus makes life itself a highpoint. If we choose to humble ourselves before the mighty hand of God and allow Him to exalt us in His timing, casting our cares on Him knowing that He cares for us, we will keep God in good and the fruit of goodness will become our melody as we worship Jesus in our day to day. Finally goodness does not come naturally but supernaturally. It is not something we do with reservation, but wholeheartedly with joy and thanksgiving. If there is no zeal in our goodness, we limit our testimony based on good times and not God's purpose and plan. Zealousness reflects a devotion to God not a promotion from God. It is a light in the darkness, a choice to become in the process of becoming. Titus 2:11-14 says, "For the grace of God has appeared, bringing salvation to all men, instructing us to deny ungodliness and worldly desires and to live sensibly, righteously and godly in the present age, looking for the blessed hope and the appearing of the glory of our great God and Savior, Christ Jesus, who gave Himself for us to redeem us from every lawless deed, and to purify for Himself a people for His own possession zealous for good deeds."

You have faith but are you faithful? The fruit of the Spirit **faithfulness** comes from the Greek word pistis, to be persuaded. Scripture says we all have been given a measure of faith, but also the freedom to choose. All trials are based on our faith and whether or not we believe that God is able and willing to provide and to meet our needs according to His riches in glory. Faithfulness is God's divine persuasion.

#932 *"Trials are the altars on which we honor God's faithfulness."*

It is the fruit of the Spirit that takes our convictions beyond our thoughts and convinces us that living for Jesus is worth it. Faithful living provides us with the assurance of things hoped for and the conviction of things not seen. It keeps us focused on God's eternal plan in the midst of temporal circumstances and disciples our souls to stay focused on rejoicing always, maintaining an attitude of prayer and giving thanks in all things.

#447 *"Faith never questions God's motives or methods."*

Remember: Faithfulness is a character quality of God. It is who God is! He is faithful to always provide for us His best in regard to His riches in glory in life. When we question God's motives, we open the door of doubt and distraction from our strongest weapon of war, worship. Our power to become relies on our willingness to believe even if it becomes difficult to understand God's methods. Proverbs 3:5 says, "Trust in the Lord with all of your heart and do not lean on your own understanding. In all of your ways acknowledge Him, and He will make your paths straight." God will never fail us; He is faithful to His word. This brings up an important aspect of sainthood, being in the word. The scripture tells us that faith comes by hearing the word of Christ. John 17:17 says, "Sanctify them in truth; Your word is truth." To be sanctified is to be set apart for God's service. When we abide in the word, we build our faithfulness and just as Jesus is faithful to His promises, we become faithful because of His promises. The truth of the word sets us free from the schemes of the enemy and holds every thought captive in obedience to Christ. Our sanctification empowers us to drown out the noise of doubt with the truth of Scripture.

#596 *"Faith is not blind, but a mindful response based on authenticated facts."*

When we walk by faith and not by sight we stop rationalizing in the flesh and start trusting in the spirit. Thanksgiving becomes an important part of our constant Christianity. It extends our faith beyond our current need and focuses on God's provisions instead of what seems to be lacking in our day to day. Our faithful perspective will keep us on the straight and narrow where trust lives. When we train our thoughts to thank God first, we will find our souls feeling the presence of God in the midst of emotional challenges.

#895 *"Victory comes when we believe that the Lord has every right to do as He pleases and trust His loving kindness to be enough."*

When faith is not applied to conviction, feeling good will take the place of a commitment to change. Talk is at its cheapest when we refer to our convictions without application. If our belief system centered on God's word is not actively producing change, we are simply doing religious calisthenics, soothing our souls but not walking in the Spirit. Hebrews 11:1 says, "Now faith is the assurance of things hoped for, the conviction of things not seen." And verse 6 says, "And without faith it is impossible to please Him, for he who comes to God must believe that He is and that He is a rewarder of those who seek Him." Faithfulness is twofold: believing that God is and a rewarder of those who seek Him. If we truly have faith, we will not be distracted by what we see. Faith goes beyond sight and trusts the fact that He who saved me is within me, and He will never leave me alone. Distance from God is only created by disobedience and disobedience is in direct relationship with disbelief. Remember: Every choice we make is based on the resurrection of Jesus. Is He alive, is He alive in me and will He ever leave me or forsake me? The foundation of God cannot be moved, it is us who have a tendency to drift. If Jesus is the anchor of your soul, believe that He is in control even when things seem out of control. Walk by faith and not by sight, let your ambition be that of pleasing God and not satisfying self. Do not question God's presence but seek His guidance in the midst of the storm.

You have gentleness, but are you gentle? **Gentleness** is power under control. Colossians 3:12 says, "So as those who have been chosen of God, holy and beloved, put on a heart of compassion, kindness, humility, gentleness and patience." As with all the fruit of the Spirit, gentleness is a choice which we make based on the truth of God's word not temporal circumstances. It is initiated by the Spirit of God and not the soul of man. Gentleness possesses no feelings of anger, fear, frustration, doubt, revenge, anxiety, or retaliation, but presents the sphere of life around you with love and forgiveness. It is established through holiness, revealed by faith and is not overwhelmed by circumstances.

#91 *"Gentleness does not speculate what could be or what might be, but stands on God's word in obedience to Christ."*

A gentle spirit is always willing to yield to the Spirit of God, is not self-seeking but instead surrendered to God's purpose and plan found in Scripture. It speaks truth with loving intent, not lording over others, but gently giving them opportunity to receive the things of God with little demand but much authority. Gentleness may be the slice of the fruit hardest to experience while taking on sainthood because it goes beyond and against everything the world, flesh and devil challenges us to become. The enemy views authority as demanding and stern, but godly authority calls us to humility and compassion. Gentleness depends on the Holy Spirit's guidance in life; it is determined to trust Jesus in spiritual growth without making demands for change. It is more concerned with the heart for change than change based on the fear of man. If we as Christians choose to possess and display a gentle spirit, our walk with Jesus will be evident and our testimony to others more effective.

#90 *"Gentleness has less to do with how others act and more to do with how we react."*

This leads to the final slice of the fruit of the Spirit, **self-control**. Self-control takes into account the full character of God and makes fruitfulness it's top priority. Self-control considers nothing but love, joy, peace, patience, kindness, goodness, faithfulness and gentleness. It is a gift from God that takes control, giving God the glory for the power to be able to experience the joy of holiness. Do not let self in self-control fool you, it has nothing to do with our ability but God's purpose and plan. It waits for teachable moments, studies God's word, does not speak inappropriately, loves unconditionally, rejoices always and in everything give thanks. Self-talk based on God's word reminds us of what is really important. It minimizes the influence of the world and helps us to make choices based on truth and not the lies of the enemy. Jesus said, you will know the truth and the truth will set you free. (John 8:32) Self-control is not a character quality that just happens, it's a determined choice that builds on Bible study, praise and prayer.

#94 *"Self-control follows after righteousness and knowledge, suggesting that what we learn should be put into practice."*

We cannot develop self-control in the midst of trials, by then it is too late. On the contrary, self-control is developed in our early morning walks and talks with Jesus, our question and answer sessions as we lie in bed at night wondering if we did our best on behalf of the King of Kings. It is in those quiet times when God's whisper is enough and our attention is completely His. When all that really matters in life is that Jesus is loved and appreciated at all times and there is no vacant areas of worship in our day to day. Self-control takes us out of the now and into eternity so that our eternal perspective will be enough to keep us free and steadfast in the moment. If you do not speak truth into your circumstances your circumstances will overwhelm you.

#150 *"Our confession will confirm God's presence and involvement in our lives or fuel the enemies attack against us."*

Too often our words are connected to our eyes and not scripture. We tend to speak based on circumstances and not faith. II Corinthians 5:7 says, "For we walk by faith, not by sight." Self-control always places us in the spirit and not the flesh. It has nothing to do with selfishness, self-centeredness, self-reliance, or self-righteousness, but instead our abiding in Jesus, learning His word and proclaiming His truth. It is the power of God in our born free position with God proclaiming the truth from God. When we are Christ- centered, we are self-controlled. We have it all: the mind of Christ, the Holy Spirit and the word of God. The power to become rests in our responsibility to control self for Christ's sake.

If we abide in Jesus and His word abides in us, the fruit of the Spirit will grow in our lives. The character of God's Spirit in us reflects the fruit of the Spirit as a whole. If the fruit is separated it becomes good works instead of God's plan. Jesus embraced all of God's character and He has given us the power to do the same, anything less is not enough.

TAKING ON SAINTHOOD

Chapter Three
Who Am I?

We have looked at how being a child of God is key to and the most important position we will ever have in the kingdom of God. As we grow in stature spiritually, emotionally and socially added spiritual responsibilities will be given to us for the purpose of discipleship. We do not leave the position of a child of God; we build on it. Our spiritual growth should take precedence over all other positions we may hold in life. The simplicity of the gospel allows us to not be overwhelmed by the business of busyness, the frailty of friends and family and the temptation of trials. When we apply wisdom from God based on our personal relationship with Jesus and our childlike faith, we set a standard of living that works in all our seasons of life.

#196 *"Four questions a humble heart asks in every circumstance: Who am I? What do I have? Who gave it to me? For what purpose?"*

Asking the question **"who am I?"** allows us to be quick to listen to the Holy Spirit's guidance, forming our words based on faith and not frustration. Preparation in the morning is not always enough for the moment. I do not have a reckless driver cutting in front of me on the freeway while I am studying the Bible over a cup of coffee, praising God for another beautiful day. But when I ask myself that question in the midst of my day to day as my soul is challenged to react emotionally and not respond spiritually, I am reminded of what is eternally important in a temporal world. Do not get me wrong, discipling the soul to respond to spiritual priorities in the morning is vital to making godly choices in the moment throughout the day. Our morning discipleship sessions prepare us for those moments, but if we do not seize the moment for God's glory the moment will seize us and our choices will be soul driven and not Spirit lead. "Who am I?" should be asked out loud and answered in the same way. You will be surprised by how quickly you will have ears to hear the Holy Spirit and a heart turned to God, not reacting to incidents but instead innocence through childlike faith. Do not wait for trials to come your way before you ask the question. Remind yourself of who you are prior to having to. You see the father of lies is always looking for opportunities to adopt you into his way of thinking. He will try to deny you your rights as a child of God by persuading you that love should be conditional and giving others what they deserve, justice. The enemy of our soul could not stop God's redemption plan, so he tries to deprive us of its power. Stay true to God's love, mercy and grace, for in doing so you will be overcomers and more than conquerors in every moment of your day.

The second question we should ask ourselves often is **"what do I have?"**. This is important because everything we have that is of any eternal value was given to us based on the birth, life, death and resurrection of Jesus. Our reality is that if we stand alone, we stand defeated. Our quality of life based on our redemption has nothing to do with good deeds done, but instead God's sufficient grace. The power invested in God's children is produced by the Holy Spirit. We have been given the power to become children of God; even our call to Christ is generated by God's Spirit, not our good intentions. So "what do we have?".

#894 "Don't be fearful by what you see physically but instead encouraged by what you know spiritually."

Let's make a list of blessings and only dwell on these throughout our day to day. First of all we have the Spirit of God. Just writing those words is humbling to me to think a holy God would send His Holy Spirit to protect and teach us how to navigate in a lost world. This blessing alone should humble us to the point of total surrender. But we have an enemy of our soul within us, the flesh. This part of man is hostile towards God, refusing to acknowledge His power and resisting the plan of redemption. Romans 8:5- 8 tells us, "For those who are according to the flesh set their minds on the things of the flesh, but those who are according to the Spirit, the things of the Spirit. For the mind set on the flesh is death, but the mind set on the Spirit is life and peace, because the mind set on the flesh is hostile toward God; for it does not subject itself to the law of God, for it is not even able to do so, and those who are in the flesh cannot please God." Galatians 5:24 says, "Now those who belong to Christ Jesus have crucified the flesh with its passions and desires." Crucifying the flesh is a lifestyle of resistance against all that is in resistance to God within us. That is why we hold every thought captive in Christ, rebuking those things that do not agree with our knowledge of God, making choices based on the truth of God's promises not the frailty of circumstances, and walking by faith and not by sight. Faith is in direct opposition to the flesh; without faith it is impossible to please God for we must believe that He is and a rewarder of those who seek Him. Through our receiving Jesus as Savior and Lord we have been given the Holy Spirit, fulfilling our sainthood. For greater is He who is in us than he that is in the world. When we are reminded of this gift from God, we will truly embrace the passion of Christ not the passion and lust of the flesh.

#881 *"When 'it is written' becomes your battle cry, your mind will be strong and your direction will be godly."*

Besides the gift of the Spirit, we have been given the word of God. Jesus said, if you abide in My word you are truly My disciples, you will know the truth and the truth will set you free. Having God's word wins the debate over the world, devil and the flesh. It is written will establish truth in the midst of the known and unknown will of God. Faith plays an important part of the hearing, receiving and acting upon that must take place when it comes to the truth of God's word. If we do not have faith in believing we will view the Bible in a novel way and not the voice of God printed on paper to express His purpose and plan for our lives. Hebrews 4:12 tells us that the word of God is alive and active, and that separates it from every other book written by man. It has nothing to do with the will or ways of man that has any significance, on the contrary it exposes man's sinfulness. The spiritual principles of God's word teaches us eternity in the midst of our temporal experience. God's word actually brings spiritual sense into an otherwise limited existence based on sight and feelings, not faith. The Bible is sharp and distinct, not vague and compromised. It clearly gives us enough of God's known will so that when the unknown comes knocking, we let Jesus answer the door. The known will of God produces an awareness in the fact that Jesus is our way, truth and spiritual life, and He is worth trusting. Actually God's word tells us not to even lean on our limited understanding but simply acknowledge the presence of Jesus and He will straighten out in our hearts and minds whatever is concerning us. The words "I don't understand" should always be replaced with "it is written". Jesus used those words before sharing spiritual truth against the lies of the devil when He was tempted in the wilderness and defeated His adversary with truth. Our enemy is very well-versed when it comes to half- truths. Do not fall for what seems to be, but instead always insert Biblical truth into the unknown in the midst of your day to day. This will keep you eternally focused and grateful. In this world, unity is more important than truth. The message of the gospel is offensive to a lost world seeking their own way. The world says can't we all get along, love is love. The Bible says God is love and unity can only be achieved when we unite with God through redemption and pursue holiness as defined in Scripture.

#297 *"God will give you the ability to please Him and expose the lies that would deprive you of that pleasure."*

God's word also separates soul from spirit. Our soul is the seat of our feelings and emotional choices. Prior to receiving Jesus we were soul driven, our choices were based on how we reflect in the moment. When the Holy Spirit entered our hearts, we realized there was a better way, disciplining the soul to trust and worship God becomes part of the maturing process. We harness our emotions to follow truth and righteousness and not to get entangled with emotional reactions based on circumstantial evidence. God's word helps us to define truth, surrendering the soul to His purpose and plan. The Bible tells us that God's divine power has granted to us everything pertaining to spiritual life and godliness through our knowledge of Jesus Christ. (II Peter 1:3) Spiritual power helps us to teach the soul to worship and not fret, to respond to and trust God's purpose and plan and not react to circumstances that would distract us and hinder our witness. Trials are inevitable, misery is optional.

Only the word of God can teach the soul of man to experience the fullness of life. David says, "Bless the Lord, O my soul, and all that is within me bless His holy name." (Psalm 103:1) Jesus echoes that same sentiment in the garden of Gethsemane, My soul is troubled to the point of death, if it is possible take this cup of redemption, the dying for the sins of man from Me, but not My will but Yours be done. A disciplined soul says God's will be done in the midst of trying emotional circumstances. Hebrews 4:12 also tells us that God's word will separate soul from spirit, joint from marrow. This is key to the term divide and conquer, the devil spends all his time trying to separate us from God's presence and His word because he knows that in doing so we rest on our laurels instead of the reverence and truth found in His presence and the scripture. When we abide in the word, we will be able to separate the mechanics of life from the essence of life. Life is not always what it seems. If we have no spiritual fortitude in our day to day, living will be one failing after another. We will live in the miseries of man not the mysteries of God and will elect an emotion to decide how we will deal with the circumstances in life instead of trusting God's will be done in the midst of trials and testing. What the Bible does for us is allow spiritual truths to overrule emotional explosions throughout our day to day. We get to use God's truth to divide and conquer. Instead of being distracted by what we see, we stand fast on who we are and who we know God is. Life should be a mysterious experience that confounds the worlds logic, opening doors of communication in regard to everything pertaining to life and godliness. The power to separate in a godly manner releases the power to become and overcome.

God's word also provides for us the ability to judge the thoughts and intentions of the heart. Scripture says as a man thinks in his heart so he is. There is a distinct connection between the mind and the heart, a mysterious connection to say the least. I am not sure how it works, maybe there is a filtering through the mind into the soul that takes place: truth from God or lies from the enemy, a world view or a born free heart setting the standard for the mind to judge righteously or satisfy self. Thoughts enter into the mind and are either held captive in obedience to Christ and rebuked out loud or allowed to enter the soul. For simplicity sake, God's word holds every thought to a holy standard of living in the aim or plan that thought represents, either God's love, mercy and grace or a self-serving reaction to people or circumstances.

#32 *"Bad choices start with one thought unchecked."*

Remember: Every word or action is initiated with a thought. We cannot say we did not mean to say it; once we act upon a thought it will always be premeditated. The truth of God's word is our prevent defense, it slows life down enough for us to make a calculated choice based on God's purpose and plan with no ungodly emotional reaction. Once we as children of God have developed a lifestyle of crucifying the flesh, discipling the soul and walking in the Spirit, these three daily exercises take place in a moment of time, realizing the mind of Christ is achievable and that the power of God is real and easily accessible by faith. II Peter 1:3 says, "Seeing that His divine power has granted to us everything pertaining to life (Zoe-Spirit) and godliness, (focus towards God) through the true knowledge of Him who called us by His own glory and excellence." We rejoice in trials because they are a test of our faith in God's omnipotence, omniscience, and omnipresence. God's almighty power is matched by no one or no thing. His wisdom and His constant presence, once believed, will create in us a trust within our hearts that cannot be defeated by a person or circumstance. When we are in Christ, we become the only person who can distract, disturb or defeat us through unbelief. It is vital that the born free spirit maintain vigilance over a childlike faith in which we build our lives on. We should not forsake the fellowshipping of the saints but we must also realize first and foremost that we are an army of one.

The third question we must ask ourselves is **"who gave me what I have?"** to become more than a conqueror in Christ. God's redemption plan gives us a life assurance policy that will form our eternal perspective in our day to day. Unconditional love releases unconditional forgiveness. If you want to get in the way of God's power attaining to life and godliness, just put limitations on your love and do not forgive the sphere of life around you. Our choices will release or deprive God's glory in our lives, everything God does is based on His love. God loved and gave us His Son Jesus as a sacrifice for our sins and redemption for our lives. (John 3:16) God's love, mercy and grace is the epitome of redemption, the forgiveness of sins. We do not have to feel love to love, it is a choice based on the power of God's love in us, extending to the sphere of life around us. It has nothing to do with the behavior of others, only the plan and purpose of God for us and through us. God's love does not expect or require love or even like in return. James

1:17-18 tells us, "Every good thing given and every perfect gift is from above, coming down from the Father of lights, with whom there is no variation or shifting shadow. In the exercise of His will He brought us forth by the word of truth, so that we would be a kind of first fruits among His creatures."

#359 *"In every process of Christian growth, love is the starting point."*

When God gave us His love and sent His Son, He gave us Himself and with that gift we have the power to become children of God, the foundation of our sainthood, and every blessing on earth as it is in heaven. Whatever the Scripture says we have been given was initiated by the gift of love. The Father has given us this perfect gift as an example of what it takes to become all that God has called us to be. It is that part of God's character that makes life happen. The Bible says that in the midst of our day to day, love casts out fear, covers a multitude of sins and never fails.

God never promised us satisfaction but contentment, knowing and believing that He is in control even when things seem out of control. Contentment involves the truth of God's word and trusting in God's plan and timing to develop God's likeness. When your heart is full of God's love, contentment is an automatic response to His presence.

Everything we have in life that is worth living for comes from our Father. Who we are is based on who God is. He did not spare His own Son, but gave Him up for us all; how will He not also with Him freely give us all things? (Romans 8:32) God not only provides us with a way when there seems no other way but gives us abundantly above and beyond that which we ask or think.

Love and forgiveness go hand-in-hand. When God loved He forgave, redemption was centered on this premise. To know that forgiveness is partnered with love should help us to not be surprised when our love is rejected or taken advantage of. God demonstrated His love for us that while we were yet sinners rejecting His love and redemption, He died for us. (Romans 5:8) A God way to prepare yourself to forgive is to love expecting nothing in return, unconditionally. Your ability to forgive will always reflect unconditional love, and the character of God. Unforgiveness has nothing to do with God's love, mercy and grace, it is simply an excuse for ungodly behavior. Unforgiveness is a soul driven choice based on what people have said or done, or circumstances beyond our control. It has nothing to do with our faith in God.

#4 "Unforgiveness is undoing what Jesus died to accomplish."

Our final question is **"for what purpose?"**. It is that we shine the light of Jesus in such a way that others acknowledge our good works and give the Father all the glory. We are sign posts that share who we are, what we have, how we got it and for what purpose. When people are interested in your Spirit-filled life and they ask the question, "what's with you?" our response should be Jesus is with me, without Him I am nothing. Our sainthood is based on Him and Him alone. We should get up every day with joy and hope in anticipation of another day spent with Jesus, moved by His Spirit, in awe of our Father. I Thessalonians 5:16-18 tells us that God's will for us is to rejoice always, pray without ceasing, and in everything give thanks. When these three areas of Christianity are happening, God things happen. We no longer live in fear or frustration controlled by our circumstances or soul driven in our choices. We praise God for who He is not for what He has done for us lately. We lead with joy by faith in Jesus Christ, who for the joy set before Him took on redemption and rose from the grave empowering us to do the same. We acknowledge who we are for the purpose of worshiping who God is. Joy may take on different forms based on the testing of our faith but will never stop happening or be influenced by challenging circumstances. Because when we choose to stay in constant communication with God, having ears to hear the Spirit's response to our prayers, rejoicing is always our first response to God's glory. Having an attitude of prayer keeps us focused on the facts of God's word, not the frailty of man's opinion or feelings. This brings us to thanksgiving, giving thanks to God knowing that His love, mercy and grace is working out His redemptive plan in our lives as a witness to the sphere of life around us. Thanksgiving rejoices in God's plan whatever that may be in our lives leaving no doubt that God will provide and that His provision is sufficient for the moment. Thanksgiving is extending our faith beyond our current needs.

The devil would like nothing better than for us to turn from Jesus and focus on ourselves, weakening our faith and magnifying our feelings. Actually God's word teaches us that God solves our problems by showing us we have no problems. We can live careless (free from anxiety) in the presence of God. Matthew 11:28-30 says, "Come to Me, all who are weary and heavy-laden and I will give you rest. Take My yoke upon you and learn from Me, for I am gentle and humble in heart, and YOU WILL FIND REST FOR YOUR SOULS. For My yoke is easy and My burden is light." When we take on the yoke of Jesus and walk hand-in-hand in stride with Him we have no cares in the world. In the midst of our concerns we realize Jesus is Lord, we are Kings kids and God will never leave us or forsake us; our Father has given us His word! Insert God whenever you say or think the word hard; for example hard times become God times, the battle belongs to the Lord, we just have to believe and trust His love, mercy and grace in the midst of hard times making them God times. The saddest thing in life is when you stop believing God has prepared a solution in the midst of trouble.

#449 *"The subject of our trials don't test us, but instead our faith in God through those trials."*

When we are yoked with Jesus, we allow our souls to rest in Christ's reality, not what we see or seems to be. Remember: God is Spirit and we worship Him in Spirit and truth. This allows us to look past the things we see and make choices based on the God we know. Taking on sainthood is walking by faith and not by sight, standing on the promises of God and not falling for the lies of the enemy. Choices will always be ours to make. If we choose self over Savior, the gravity of sin will always take us down, but the gentleness of Jesus elevates us above and beyond our current needs. This allows us to do God's will on earth as it is in heaven, just like Jesus did when He walked on earth.

TAKING ON SAINTHOOD

Chapter Four

Relationship or Religion

When Jesus came to earth, He put an end to religion and opened for us communication directly with the Father. Everything changed on earth as it was in heaven. Mankind trying in vain to appease their gods through good works and sacrifice were given an opportunity to receive God's unmerited favor through His Son Jesus Christ. Even the Jews who served Jehovah the only true God, whom He chose as a holy nation to birth Christ, became caught up in their own religious laws, becoming outlaws in regard to our Father's redemptive plan. All of us since Eden are born into religion, our sin keeps us religious. When Jesus spoke of doing His Father's will and work, it was the first time God was viewed as a personal God, wanting a relationship with man. John 14:6 says, "I am the way, and the truth, and the life; no one comes to the Father but through Me." This statement was offensive to the religious leaders of the time because it denounced their position and privilege putting all mankind on an even plane, all needing Jesus, God's gift of redemption, leading to relationship with the Father.

No one is born in right relationship with God. Our religious sin is self-interest. It may involve a desire to seek God or not, but without receiving Jesus into our hearts, self will stay on the throne and good works will be our justification for not needing God's love, mercy and grace through the life, death and resurrection of Jesus Christ. The flesh in itself is self-righteous and finds no reason to surrender to God's holiness. Man's religion from birth is self-reliance and arrogance that rejects everything pertaining to God, and just as the religious leaders that led the attack against Jesus leading to His crucifixion, it does not want to relinquish its position and privilege in this world.

#81 *"The flesh doubts God's ability, and in doing so doubts God's word, and in doing so doubts God's character, and in doing so doubts God's existence."*

Taking on sainthood relinquishes every position and privilege in our society to the position of child of God. If we do not view life on an even field, we could find ourselves lording over those very people in our sphere of life that God has called us to serve as unto the Lord. It is so much easier to be abrupt than patient and compassionate. A strong hand is not better than a loving heart. A child of God takes on the yoke of Jesus and applies that same yoke to the sphere of life around them, giving no high ground to any position of authority or responsibility. Throughout the Old Testament the consistent failure that is revisited over and over are the kings failing to tear down the high places. These were altars serving false gods. Too often our position and privilege become similar altars that if not torn down in humble surrender to Jesus, become stumbling blocks that hinder God's purpose. Religious behavior in the midst of our relationship with Jesus is an easy slip that can be avoided if we once again remember that all our thoughts, words and deeds flow from God's power to become children of God. Being born religious is a hard thing to overcome in this world. I Corinthians 1:18 says, "For the word of the cross is foolishness to those who are perishing, but to us who are being saved it is the power of God." Through Christ all things are possible and in Christ all things are powerful. There is a reason Jesus did not come to earth as a prince or king. The frailty and faithfulness of a child in a manger teaches us the way God desires us to live. Our redemption was established that night in Bethlehem and was built upon throughout the different stages of growth and responsibility that Jesus experienced on His way to Calvary and eventually Easter morning.

The power to become children of God is based on His story and every chapter of His life reflects Bethlehem's frailty and faithfulness in His Father, who is now our Father through Jesus Christ.

#299 *"If it is inspired by God's Spirit, if it is confirmed in God's word, if it involves God's best, it is not impossible."*

So yes, the world sees relationship with God as foolish and the cross as unnecessary, but God's chosen people, known from birth to be born again, see God for who God is. The choice to build a relationship with the Father through Jesus makes all the difference in our world. I do not understand the mystery of being chosen by God, but in the midst of life, God gives us all opportunity to be redeemed by the blood and filled by His Spirit. It is the whosoever in John 3:16 that makes that clear. Why me and not you is not clear, but my question to you is why not you? Other than a deliberate choice to stay self-righteous, religious and god of your world, it makes little sense. We have no power or hope when we are god, only temporal pockets of satisfaction that seem to vanish as quickly as they appear.

#33 *"A disciple is someone who arranges his or her life and surroundings to give God maximum freedom to achieve His goals."*

Peace is not the absence of conflict but the presence of God. It cannot be attained in this world; it comes from an outside source, a divine presence that was instituted when the Prince of Peace appeared as a child. Trouble and fear will always enter in where God's peace, Jesus, is denied. It is important to understand that even though we may have chosen Jesus at some point in our lives, slipping into religious behavior is always a temptation. Taking control of our position and privilege will always lead to trouble and fear. Make no excuse, when you are on the throne Jesus is not and God's presence is no longer your peace. You seek after those pockets of satisfaction in the midst of your happenings instead of choosing to rejoice always, maintaining an attitude of prayer and in everything giving thanks. Happiness only comes when you have settled the joy of the Lord in your heart. Happy is the man whose God is the Lord. How do we avoid these lapses into religion? Trust and communication are keys to building strong relationships. Remember: The subject of our trials do not test us, but instead our faith in God through those trials. If we try to understand the circumstances life produces, we will find ourselves frustrated and distracted. Faith causes us to live our lives based on the facts of the word, not the frailty of circumstances.

#84 *"Faith convinces us of what is true without physical evidence."*

Trust is accepting God's plan for our lives even when His purpose seems impossible to understand. It is a spiritual act that refuses to be unfaithful to a loving God based on who God is, not what circumstances seem to be. If we need an example of trust, we need look no further than Jesus' trust in the Father. John 14:10 says, "…The words that I say to you I do not speak on My own initiative, but the Father abiding in Me does His works." Every thought, word and deed of Christ was initiated by the Father. So as we abide in Christ and His word abides in us, we should speak not on our own initiative, but so that the Father's works be fulfilled. This is where communication becomes an important part of relationship building. Jesus said if you abide in My word you are truly My disciples, you will know the truth and the truth will set you free. (John 8:31-32) Constant Christianity means constant communication. We speak to God in prayer, God speaks to us through His word. Revelation does happen by the Holy Spirit, but God usually speaks to us through rhema, the Greek word used to describe a spoken word from the pages of scripture. Whenever we have a communication breakdown it is never God's fault. It is interesting that in

Philippians 4:4-6 the term "the Lord is near" is sandwiched between "Rejoice in the Lord always" and "be anxious for nothing". The term the Lord is near in the Greek means in place of time. So Jesus at any moment can replace time if we let Him. He can place love to cast out fear, peace that surpasses understanding to replace any anxious moment and provide us with hope, that joyful anticipation of God doing something special in our lives. If we do not seize the moment the moment will seize us; anxiety will flood our soul and fear will inject its venomous thoughts challenging God's love for us. Knowing God's word brings understanding to the known will of God, accepting the unknown will of God. When Jesus said, you will know the truth and the truth will set you free, He was telling us that God's eternal truth must be our reality.

#121 "Wherever emotions rule there is no faith."

Too often we as Christians get caught up in the visual concept of life and not God's eternal plan. We see with the flesh and not the spirit. God's word trains us to view life from an eternal perspective with holiness as our goal. If we could imagine God speaking every time we read the Bible, it would remind us of how much the Father wants intimacy. Do not just read the Bible, study the heart of the Father and listen to the Spirit's voice speaking through each page. Relationship is trusting and relating to one another from the heart. Any doubt is a thought rebuked and replaced with the truth of God's word.

When we are in righteous relationship with the Father all things will work for the good, life will be easy and carefree and God's glory will rest upon us and all that we say and do. Consistency will make all the difference in our walk with Jesus. If we as Christians want to leave a legacy in this world, we must determine to be constant and consistent when it comes to our love and submission to Christ. I prefer not to have God put up with my soul driven choices or love me in spite of my self-righteous perspective. I want to rejoice more and repent less and walk in the Spirit of Christ. We cannot get any more of the Holy Spirit, but the Holy Spirit can surely get more of us. You cannot lose if your mind is set on spiritual gain.

#761 "The difference between a saint and a sinner is what they practice."

We should not only view Scripture as God speaking to us but memorize Scripture as God speaking through us. Isn't it interesting how children can memorize with ease, but as they get older it takes much more effort on their part. So it is with a child of God. At first our faith assures us that the word is vital to our existence, and we love and want to know Him and the power of His word, so we memorize, always mimicking His every word and deed. So what happens in life that causes us to choose ignorance over knowledge? I believe we take on position and privilege, a God thing when kept holy under the guidance of scripture with a personal relationship with Jesus as it's priority. But if our position and privilege becomes self-seeking, we are back where this chapter begins, even worse. To be born self-righteous is one thing but to choose self- righteousness after experiencing the presence and power of God is deadly. God owes us nothing yet He chose to give us everything pertaining to life in the Spirit and a focus towards Him. His word is who God is and when He chose to become the spoken word of God all hell broke loose and heaven on earth was established. I believe the devil thought he finally rid himself of the Word became flesh on Calvary. He was not expecting Easter when the Word was alive never to be bound again by the sin of man.

#712 *"Don't be bound by the grave when Jesus rose from it."*

Jesus rose from the grave and defeated death and dying, but He also established eternal living. In Him was life and His life was the Light of men and to as many as received Him, to them He gave the power to become children of God. (John 1) The devil, world and flesh wants to stop the word of God within us, working through us. Taking on sainthood is about obedience to the Word made flesh. That is the position of privilege that makes all the difference in the world. Take off the grave clothes of self-righteousness, self-satisfaction and self-seeking and humble yourself before the mighty hand of God, casting all your cares on Him and He will exalt you at the proper time.

One of the challenges we face in sainthood is humility and being exalted at the proper time. According to I Peter 5, the proper time is when Jesus comes again in all His glory, so do not let your flesh get all excited in the now. What we get to do on this earth is humble ourselves, serve according to God's will, proving to be examples to the sphere of life around us, casting anxiety on Jesus who cares more about us than we care about Him, being sober in Spirit, resisting the devil. And through God's grace we will be perfected, confirmed, strengthened and established in Christ after we have suffered for a little while. Just as Jesus told His disciples He must die but will rise again, God's word tells us clearly what God's known will for us will be. And if we have faith and believe God's word we will not be caught off guard, but instead be fully armored with truth and His Spirit to be more than conquerors in a world unable to make spiritual sense with its temporal perspective. We must walk in the power to become long before the need to overcome is necessary. This is because God's known will and our faith is enough to walk in victory in a defeated world steeped with religion.

#115 *"You know when someone is hearing with prejudice, they reiterate the problem instead of proclaiming the promise."*

Listening is an important part of building relationships. James 1:19 tells us to be quick to listen, slow to speak and slow to anger, for the anger of man does not achieve the righteousness of God. We either hear with purpose or with prejudice. When we approach God's word with preconceived opinions that are not based on spiritual reason or godly experience, we limit if not block the Holy Spirit's ability to liberate our souls and empower our spirits. Scripture teaches us God's will so that we can accomplish His purpose for our lives. When we read with purpose, we hear the truth pertaining to God's will based on our experience with Jesus, and take His promises to heart and not with a grain of salt. The art of listening does not come naturally but supernaturally. We must study to show ourselves approved by God, not for the sake of others approval or for any selfish gain. If we have ears to hear what the Spirit is speaking and hearts to believe God's promises are necessary instructions for our day to day, we will resolve in our hearts that God is able to meet all our needs according to His riches in glory. He solves our problems by showing us we have no problems to worry about, only promises to brag about.

#110 *"If we are truly God's children, we are ruled by His will and made joyful by His presence."*

A child of God is convinced that God's presence is real and His will is worth living for. This position and privilege creates the joy of the Lord which is our strength. So if you find yourself reiterating the problems in life, repent for your prejudice and lack of faith in God's plan and begin to proclaim with praise and thanksgiving the promises of God's word that brings power over yesterday, today and forever. Remember: Our confession will train our minds. When we hold every thought captive in obedience to Christ, we need also to confess the promises of God's word that will fulfill His purpose in its place. Your mind will begin to dwell on the blessings of God and not the challenges of this world. Thoughts may be random but they can also be purposeful if we discipline our minds to dwell on who we know God is and not be swayed by doubt or despair.

TAKING ON SAINTHOOD

Chapter Five

Sainthood

From the beginning of time God's plan has been for us to be saints; holy ones called and commissioned to do God's work, to live holy, and worship Him in Spirit and truth. The Greek word holy in scripture, hagios, is used to describe purity, sanctification, holiness and saint. You cannot separate holy from saint, it is who God's children become when Jesus is received, believed and obeyed. The word saint is referred to in Scripture as a believer of Jesus. Saint is first used in Matthew 27:52 when, after Jesus yielded up His Spirit, the temple veil was torn from top to bottom, the earth quaked, the tombs were opened and the saints who had fallen asleep or died were raised and entered the holy city and appeared to many. In short, saints have resurrection power that is directly related to God's redemptive plan.

#1060 *"Sainthood or holiness is not something we achieve but a position we embrace."*

I Peter 1:16 says, "...YOU SHALL BE HOLY, FOR I AM HOLY." Saints are bound and determined to accept and build on the premise of holiness. We have no holiness in ourselves but once Jesus becomes Savior and Lord, all of God's power to become holy children of God is at our disposal. And like everything given to us by God it is free, but only faithful application of it in our lives will prove its power. In I Peter 1:13-23, Peter gives us building blocks that establish God's holiness in our day to day. Remember: At no point is holiness achieved based on our good deeds, it is a gift from God necessary for salvation. Holiness replaces sinfulness and His story replaces and establishes our history. Even our good works as a light in a dark world are so that others may glorify the Father who is in heaven. (Matthew 5:16) Good works are only made possible through the fact that we are sanctified by the blood of Jesus. A simple definition of sanctification is being set apart for God's service. Nothing in our carnal self can achieve or accomplish what Jesus provided on Calvary. It is only our spirit in communion with Christ that presents us to the Father justified and holy. Paul writes in I Corinthians 1:26-31, "For consider your calling, brethren, that there were not many wise according to the flesh, not many mighty, not many noble; but God has chosen the foolish things of the world to shame the wise, and God has chosen the weak things of the world to shame the things which are strong, and the base things of the world and the despised God has chosen, the things that are not, so that He may nullify the things that are, so that no man may boast before God. But by His doing you are in Christ Jesus, who became to us wisdom from God, and righteousness and sanctification, and redemption, so that, just as it is written, 'LET HIM WHO BOASTS, BOAST IN THE LORD'." It is clear in scripture that our accomplishments are based on God's power not of our own doing.

#340 *"Holiness means submission to Christ, obedience to His word, surrender to His spirit and service to all."*

So as we look at the building blocks in I Peter 1:13-23, keep in mind your sanctification, and let your boast be of the Lord alone. The first building block Peter tells us is **to prepare our minds for action**; a thoughtless mind is unprepared for battle. Saints possess the mind of Christ, always thinking of ways to worship the Father and serve others. An active mind holds every thought captive in obedience to Christ and judges those thoughts in the Spirit of godly knowledge, not circumstantial evidence. Remember: Our thoughts precede our words and actions. When our minds are vacant the flesh will fill it with self- satisfying, self-serving, self-righteous thoughts leading to ungodly soul driven choices. Filling your mind with God's word produces the mind of Christ. Truth and trials create testimonies of God's faithfulness. When we prepare our minds for action we must believe that God's word is worth thinking about and without it we have no power.

#459 *"Preparation never stops, sobriety never ends and our hope of glory will always be achieved when it is all said and done."*

When it comes to God's word there are no seasons of growth. Constant Christianity takes pleasure in knowing the truth and sharing the spoken word with others daily. If you are standing still you are falling behind and missing the point. A saint lives holy through daily preparation and purposeful choices that will equip both them and others with thought-provoking principles of God's word. Everything we say and do should be an overflow of a mind prepared for action.

The second building block is **keep sober in spirit**; the last thing this world needs is a drunk saint intoxicated with blurred vision and a compromised heart. A sober spirit sees things from God's perspective-it does not weaken it's resolve with worldly sedatives that lead to dissipation. You will never waste time when you focus on God's timing in the midst of a storm. Staying calm is a true sign of a sober spirit. A sober spirit is anxious for nothing, but in everything gives thanks in prayer and petition resulting in a peace that surpasses understanding. A spirit that is intoxicated with the world and flesh behaves irrationally, lacking self-control, forming soul driven choices and not Spirit led decisions. Its timing is more important than God's and worry takes the place of worship. When we choose holiness over happenings we decide to allow the presence of God to control our presence of mind. Our sobriety becomes priority in our day to day and temperate living our lifestyle. Preparation once again is key to living the life of a saint. Sobriety comes when we abide in the word knowing its truth and experiencing liberty in Christ. A daily choice to become empowers us before the temptation to be intoxicated overpowers us. Saints are filled with the Spirit and walk with steadfastness as they navigate the trials and temptations set before them. When someone becomes a saint, hope is restored and self-satisfaction is exchanged for godly contentment.

The third building block is **hope**, the joyful anticipation that God is at work and His timing is perfect. I Peter 1:13 tells us to hope completely on the grace to be brought to us at the revelation of Jesus Christ. Hope is that faithful confidence in knowing that God is in control even when everything seems out of control. Our sainthood is flawed if we are waiting to rejoice based on our circumstances. You do not ever wait to rejoice; you rejoice in the midst of waiting.

#1132 "Hope leads with joy and is founded in love."

Joy should be our go to fruit of the Spirit that we nibble on daily. Hope is not hope if rejoicing is not part of it. We have three basic forms of joy that we choose to embrace throughout our lives in anticipation of God's grace through a revelation of Jesus Christ. The first joy is cheerfulness, a standard practice of a believer. It should be reflected in our countenance, attitude and perspective. Being cheerful for one reason, and one reason alone, the presence of Jesus, tells the sphere of life around us that Jesus is alive and worthy to be praised. The second form of joy is a calm delight. This is a joy that expresses hope in the midst of trials; it also is reflected in our countenance, attitude and perspective, but in a more subdued manner. A calm delight walks with Jesus in the storms of life, never questioning God's purpose and plan and always giving testimony of God's faithfulness no matter what challenges we face. It is detached from the world and divinely displays hope in God's grace. The third form of joy is exceeding joy. This happens when miraculous healing takes place in any form, physical, spiritual, relational, financial, etc. It is a jumping up and down joy that we enjoy the most but should be equal to its counterparts. Cheerfulness, calm delight and exceeding joy should be displayed in one form or another throughout our journey. There is nothing hopeless in sainthood, just a joyful anticipation of God fulfilling His love for us through His Spirit that was given to us. (Romans 5:5)

#600 *"The world walks in the futility of their minds, instead of the purity of their hearts."*

Obedience is the next building block in sainthood. Prior to our new birth we were ignorant to the truth and unable to live holy by faith. But when we responded to the call of the Spirit and received Jesus into our hearts, purity became our desire and faith our supernatural response to God. There is a direct correlation to believing and obeying. It is important that we believe in order to avoid conforming back to the futility of our minds. Transformation is consistent with sainthood. When we trust and obey we walk in faith and holiness, no longer conforming to ignorance, but transforming through wisdom. Saints are always tempted to ignore the simplicity of the gospel and to allow thoughts to drift away from Jesus, leaving us with self-doubt and confusion. Choosing to believe and obey rebukes such temptations, leaving us strong and godly in our thoughts, words and deeds.

#893 *"Faith is the only thing that gives God His proper place in our lives, and is the only thing that lifts our souls above the influence of circumstances."*

The next building block is a mysterious one to say the least, but it is necessary to experience life in the Spirit. The **fear of the Lord** is that building block of sainthood that draws us to Jesus and keeps us focused on eternity. His fear is both an awesome reverence of God and a dreadful reality of what our lives would look like without Him. That is where the mystery lies, a holy God who carved out a moment in time to redeem us from our sins, to be holy as He is holy, yet unable to save us if we choose to reject His love. When we embrace the fear of the Lord in Christ we are covered by the blood, filled with the Spirit and given everything pertaining to life and godliness including a free will to choose God's loving kindness daily. When we sin we have repentance as a tool to restore us to holiness. The fear of the Lord should be embraced because it is our reality in life, a reminder of what is and what could be. Jesus established what could be on Calvary, the horror of the cross redeeming those who believe as holy. The pain, misery and shame of sin against the Father, Jesus bore in His body and soul, the Father's justice was satisfied and sin no longer ruled in our lives. Our reverent awe of a loving God should be a reminder of His sacrifice for the forgiveness of our sins, never lording over us but instead mercifully serving us in our weakness and guiding us with love throughout our day to day. Proverbs 19:23 tells us, "The fear of the Lord leads to life, so that one may sleep satisfied, untouched by evil." Remember: The Holy Spirit works through the fear of the Lord, His Spirit is what leads us to fear Him for the sake of spiritual life and our focus towards God. When we sleep we are at peace, not satisfied because we were not tempted, tested or challenged through the day, but spiritually content, knowing that we are on the right side of redemption; God calling us to Himself from the beginning of time to live holy and productive lives for His glory. Our faith and believing the fear of the Lord is essential for life, protecting us from the lies of the devil and establishing our saintly position in a lost world. Living in a fear that leads to death denies our Savior, Jesus Christ. Holiness proceeds power and faith proceeds holiness.

#650 *"Faith precedes purity, if you don't believe a pure heart is conceivable, you won't totally commit to it."*

It will always come back to faith, the assurance policy that frees us to trust and obey. The worlds faith is seeing is believing, God's faith is the assurance of things hoped for the conviction of things not seen. Sainthood is experiencing life from God's perspective, to dwell in the source of all true pleasure and to enjoy life as God Himself would and as Jesus did. As we close this chapter, let's remember these three things: a pure heart has one interest, one loyalty and one perspective, to worship God more fully, serve God more effectively and see His purpose and plan more clearly. Being totally committed to worship is a true sign of saintly behavior. When we worship God for who God is and not for what He can do for us our motives will be pure with no change of circumstances necessary. Let's get into the habit of praising Jesus for nothing, no strings attached, no ulterior motives. Whether it be a trial or temptation, a pure heart will see God at work to will and to do according to His good pleasure in Christ. Answered prayer should never be the basis of our worship and thanksgiving.

Psalms 34:1-4 says, "I will bless the Lord at all times; His praise shall continually be in my mouth. My soul will make its boast in the Lord; the humble will hear it and rejoice. O magnify the Lord with me, and let us exalt His name together. I sought the Lord, and He answered me, and delivered me from all my fears."

When we worship God in everything, He builds our faith in His love and casts out all fear in our day to day.

TAKING ON SAINTHOOD

Chapter Six

Answering the Call

From the beginning of time, while we were yet in our mothers wombs, God has called us to Himself. His one desire is to have a relationship with us and to reflect His glory through us. We who are called benefit from His love, mercy and grace throughout our day to day and testing becomes our testimony and trials our triumphs. God's call is not a one-time experience but instead a lifestyle of spiritual goals given to us through His word, equipping us for sanctification, being set apart and holy for God's service, worshiping Him and witnessing to the sphere of life around us. Holiness is God's standard of living for us and as we take on sainthood, answering the call of God is essential for us to be complete, lacking in nothing. Romans 8:28 says, "And we know that God causes all things to work together for good to those who love God, to those who are called according to His purpose."

#396 *"Live each day of your life on purpose with purpose."*

Wherever you are for whatever given time you are there, you are part of God's purpose and plan for your life. Let us be clear, God is not a sadistic father who takes pleasure in our pain. On the contrary, His purpose in the midst of tribulation is to redeem the time and restore our healing. The path to heaven may take us through some difficult terrain but fear not Jesus tells us in John 16:33 "…I have overcome the world."

God's purpose is first and foremost spiritual, and where the Spirit of the Lord is there is liberty. Our freedom to overcome is based on our never losing sight of our eternal position as children of God as we go through temporal circumstances. Trials will never define God's purpose in our lives.

Our faith in Him will not only define His purpose but also determine our witness. So yes, God causes everything to work for the good and His purpose is found throughout our trials and triumphs. God's purpose is His blessed assurance in difficulties and delays that He cares and will never leave us or forsake us.

#926 *"Every day is a blessing from God, take advantage of all the growth it provides."*

Answering the call to worship instead of our human tendency to worry is part of our process to become, knowing that God not only calls us to worship, He empowers us too. Anything pertaining to the process of becoming is empowered by God's Spirit and worship is our spiritual gift from God that demonstrates our love and gratitude towards Him. When worship is our first instinct internally, the temporal becomes dimmed compared to His glory in life, so rejoice always, in everything give thanks for that is God's will in Christ. (I Thessalonians 5:18) It is important to take worship from our song service and into our day to day. It is easy to discipline our souls compartmentally, that is to connect our emotional response to God's blessings based on where we are instead of who we are. God has called us to always and never, that is constant Christianity. We always praise, pray, prepare and never fear, doubt or distance ourselves from Him. You may say I cannot do that, that statement in itself perks up the ears of the devil and weakens our determination and hinders the power in Christ to become. Your opinion of yourself makes a difference only if your opinion is based on what God's word says about you.

#434 *"Opinions are nice, but divine revelation is necessary."*

Scripture says all things are possible through Christ who strengthens you, you are more than conquerors, the righteousness of God in Christ and most of all, you are loved. If we place worship somewhere instead of everywhere we will not be spiritually connected when we need it most. Every thought producing a word, resulting in an action, should be worship to God and a witness to others. If we do all things as unto the Lord we will not wait for a church service to rejoice. Worship is not allowing anything or anyone to hinder God's progress in our lives. Worship does not come before or after trials but during them; worship should not be a part of repentance but a song of deliverance. The call to worship is a lifestyle of godliness in a godless world. So enjoy the journey, make every moment count and in all things give thanks.

The call to service is the overflow of worship. We demonstrate our faith and show our love for the Father through worship and the call to serve reflects that same faith and love to the sphere of life around us.

Matthew 22:37–40, "And He said to him, 'YOU SHALL LOVE THE LORD YOUR GOD WITH ALL YOUR HEART, WITH ALL YOUR SOUL, AND WITH ALL YOUR MIND.'

This is the great and foremost commandment. The second is like it, 'YOU SHALL LOVE YOUR NEIGHBOR AS YOURSELF.' On these two commandments depend the whole Law and the Prophets."

The Bible addresses two important positions in this world: One before God and the other before man. Wholeness, being all that God has called us to be and witness, reflecting that call to the sphere of life around us. We are to live holy and in doing so, serve others as Christ served us in redemption.

#335 *"If you have a heart for God, you will have a heart for God's people, even those who don't know Him yet."*

When we take on sainthood we have been given will power through the Holy Spirit, the power to fulfill God's will in our lives. God not only calls us, but enables us to fulfill our calling. Our Father will never enlist us for service without giving us the power to fulfill our commission. Jesus says in John 15:16 "You did not choose Me but I chose you, and appointed you that you would go and bear fruit, and that your fruit would remain, so that whatever you ask of the Father in My name He may give to you." Here lies the mystery of God's positioning and power; it is Spirit based, Spirit led and Spirit provided. Every prayer offered to God should be followed with not my will but Yours be done. This says here is my temporary need or want, but I am submitted to Your spiritual purpose and plan for this moment. We should always trust God if His purpose vetoes our plans. Our prayers should be seeking God's will in the midst of our needs; that is where peace and contentment reign. Pray in the Spirit and you will never be disappointed.

#493 *"Love is strenuous and not for the faint hearted."*

The call to service is duplicating God's love that was demonstrated by Jesus on the earth. Answered prayer was never the goal of Jesus, obedience to the Father's will was. The service of love was key to the fulfillment of redemption and our service answers that call. So whatever you do, do in the name of the Lord, serve others as unto Jesus Himself. Jesus came to this earth to serve, and servitude should be the supernatural overflow of our relationship with Him.

The call to prayer involves God's desire for us to be in communication with Him without ceasing. Having an attitude of prayer is receiving the Father's advice as priority in every circumstance. Unconditional love produces unconditional trust, releasing unconditional prayer. Circumstances should never lead us to pray, God wants us to communicate with Him for no reason but love. Prayers should not be our 911 call to Jesus, but instead our daily, moment by moment love language reflecting our trust in His presence and power in His plan for our lives. Bible study releases God's communication with His saints; our prayer time is our communication with Him. These are two important steps, the call to be in His word provides us with the truth narrative necessary for us to have a meaningful conversation with the Father. When we pray scriptural truth we are praying God's spiritual language. If we don't know the principles of life found in scripture we will have difficulty speaking from our heart and our prayers will be soul driven and not Spirit lead. Soul driven prayers are emotionally based and prioritize certainty over faith. There is a strong connection between the word of God and our words to God. If you want to add to your vocabulary in prayer, begin to quote scripture for no reason other than to train your mind and disciple your soul to focus on God's will for your life. The Bible tells us faith comes by hearing and hearing the words of Christ. Life assurance is found in God's communication with us and applied in our communication with God.

#897 *"If you aren't praying daily you're not preparing for your future."*

Once our prayers have less to do with our wants and more to do with spiritual matters of the heart will we realize that God meets all of our needs according to His riches in glory in Christ Jesus. Communication and trust are necessary for any relationship to grow and prosper. When there is a communication breakdown the wiring becomes faulty and trust short circuits, creating an atmosphere in which fear and doubt can easily take over and create a new narrative other than love and truth. Feelings do count, that is why it is so important for us to discipline our souls to surrender to God's Spirit and the truth of God's word. David, in Psalm 103:1 said, "Bless the Lord, O my soul, and all that is within me, bless His holy name." His soul was obviously contrary to God's purpose and plan in the moment, his soul is telling him to feel one way and his spirit another. When we teach our souls to embrace the compassion of God and trust Him, our communication with God will be in unity with the truth of God. II Timothy 1:7 tells us that the Lord has not given to us the spirit of fear but of love, power and a disciplined mind. Knowing that our mind is the gatekeeper of the soul, we are reminded that fear begins with a thought that seeps into our souls, the seat of our choices. But when we allow the love of Jesus to flow in our hearts it casts out the spirit of fear, destroying fearful thoughts, teaching our soul to realize how much it is loved and protected. The feelings of peace and security are restored and an eternal, godly perspective is once again our main source of comfort in the midst of trying times, whether that be testing or tempting.

#629 *"It is better to cry out to God before temptation than to cry out to God after temptation has had its way."*

Psalm 5:1-3 says, "Give ear to my words, O Lord, consider my groaning. Heed the sound of my cry for help, my King and my God, for to You I pray. In the morning, O Lord, You will hear my voice; in the morning I will order my prayer to You and eagerly watch." David teaches us how to prepare for the day through prayer. He asked for help before help was needed and prays for nothing before prayer is necessary. The call to prayer involves God speaking to us through His word and our speaking to God out of reverence and gratitude for who God is, not for what He needs to do. This prepares our heart, soul and mind to glorify God in all things.

#757 "The Bible gives us divine truth and prayer allows us to have intimate conversation with the author of that truth."

There are many calls that God sets before us; we have only scratched the surface of what God desires us to embrace as necessary in the midst of our journey to heaven. But let's finish this chapter with **the call to lead**. Followers of Christ make the best leaders of men. We become leaders the moment we receive Jesus in our hearts and choose to follow Him as He leads us to heaven in a world filled with teachable moments. In Acts 4:12, Peter makes this proclamation, speaking of Jesus, "And there is salvation in no one else; for there is no other name under heaven that has been given among men by which we must be saved." That is how a leader leads, Jesus represents God's redemptive plan for mankind. Our call to lead should reflect salvation in Christ throughout our day to day. Peter makes one of the most profound statements in scripture yet his credibility had nothing to do with education or training, the only recognition he had was that he had been with Jesus. Our call to lead begins with our willingness to sit at the feet of Jesus and learn from Him. We do not need a seminar on leadership, we simply need a heart for followship. Without followship there is no fellowship; loving Jesus, serving others before satisfying self. A willing heart is all God needs to impact the sphere of life around us; God's power comes with each calling. The enemy's attack against our leadership usually deals with him trying to convince us that we are unworthy, inadequate and our voice should be silenced because of our sin. Blamelessness is the rebuke we possess in regard to these three areas of his attack. Are we practicing righteousness and getting better at it in spite of sin in our lives? Do the thoughts we think, the words we speak and our actions reflect worship that echoes worthy are You Lord to receive glory, honor and praise? Are we walking in the Spirit and not carrying out the desires of the flesh? The devil will accuse us day and night, whether we are living righteous or not. The question is are we validating the attack of the devil through our behavior or are we standing fast in the liberty wherefore Christ has set us free and choosing not to be in entangled again with the yoke of bondage, but walking in the yoke of Jesus, exposing the enemies lies and rebuking his feeble attempt to once again capture our souls through guilt and shame?

#751 *"It is better to be first to rejoice than quick to repent."*

The power of repentance is a gift from God that cleans the slate and allows God to purify our lives through the journey. But do not let it become your go to plan; lenience precedes license. We should always lead with worship in our day to day. As leaders we set the standard high and achievable according to God's Spiritual power that motivates us to holiness. Faith over feelings is our perspective as leaders that keep us in the now and forever when it comes to trials and temptations. Walking in the Spirit and not being soul driven answers the call to lead, setting an example as how to follow Jesus side by side. His yoke is easy and His burden is light.

Chapter Seven
For His Glory

These three words, "For His Glory", sum up everything pertaining to life and godliness. We do what we do because God is, and nothing else matters. First of all let's define glory as the visual presence of God. When we glorify Jesus in our day to day He is visible in the choices we make. The Fruit of the Spirit is visible, forgiveness is visible, love, grace and mercy are visible. We become a reflection of God's redemptive plan to the sphere of life around us. "For His Glory" is a statement of faith that answers the question, am I faithful? It has nothing to do with circumstances, yet everything to do with how we react to circumstances or better yet how we respond to God in the midst of circumstances. "For His Glory" is not about prayer but believing God's purpose and plan is more important than our wants, without a doubt.

#779 "God is good even when sickness doesn't disappear, finances remain a struggle, people continue to make life difficult and life remains a walk by faith and not a walk in the park."

God is good is a fact and does not need validation from God's yeses in our life. When we are committed to live life for His glory life itself takes on a different meaning; God's will becomes our wants and everything we do is unto the Lord. The word of God is our constant reminder that God is worthy of our worship and in Christ we have been given the power to be agents of His glory. God's word also reminds us that our success and failure is part of our human condition and that His love, mercy and grace keeps us humble in our success and brings restoration in our failing. God knows we are not perfect, but He also knows that not pursuing excellence in our lives will hinder our willpower and cause us to settle for less than His glory. II Corinthians 5:17 says, "Therefore if anyone is in Christ, he is a new creature; the old things passed away; behold, new things have come." We will spend our whole life battling the flesh in regard to old things and a constant reminder by the word helps us to overcome ourselves for Christ's sake. Jesus is referred to as our justification, simply put, because of Jesus we stand before the Father just as if we have not sinned. Unfortunately our old ways are centered on excuses as to why we do the things we shouldn't and don't do the things that we should. People and circumstances become our justification, not the blood of Jesus on Calvary. Remember: An excuse is the skin of reason covering a lie. Holy justification empowers us to make mistakes but persevere in God's grace through them, learning life's lessons through our failings and not making the same mistakes again. Without God's word we will be limited to our own reasoning and the opinions of the lost. When we walk in the Spirit and the new things found in God's word through Christ, we make choices to put on the full armor of God.

Ephesians 6:11-18 tells us to "Put on the full armor of God, so that you will be able to stand firm against the schemes of the devil. For our struggle is not against flesh and blood, but against the rulers, against the powers, against the world forces of this darkness, against the spiritual *forces* of wickedness in the heavenly *places*. Therefore, take up the full armor of God, so that you will be able to resist in the evil day, and having done everything, to stand firm. Stand firm therefore, HAVING GIRDED YOUR LOINS WITH TRUTH, and HAVING PUT ON THE BREASTPLATE OF RIGHTEOUSNESS, and having shod YOUR FEET WITH THE PREPARATION OF THE GOSPEL OF PEACE; in addition to all, taking up the shield of faith with which you will be able to extinguish all the flaming arrows of the evil one. And take THE HELMET OF SALVATION, and the sword of the Spirit, which is the word of God.

With all prayer and petition pray at all times in the Spirit, and with this in view, be on the alert with all perseverance and petition for all the saints."

#882 *"Remove one piece of the armor of God and you weaken your stand in Christ; truth, righteousness, the preparation of the gospel, faith, the mind of Christ, the word of God and prayer."*

The breast plate of righteousness guards our heart, truth guards our witness, the gospel of peace guards our walk in the Spirit, faith guards ungodly thoughts, saving grace guards against the temptation to stand alone, and God's word and prayer guards us from the lies of the enemy through truth found in Scripture and a constant communication with God, setting His purpose and plan before us at all times. And just as the fruit of the Spirit found in Christ is one for God's glory, so is the armor of God. Old things always hinder God's glory by picking and choosing what is convenient and comfortable. When the full armor is put on and remains on as a lifestyle and not a fashion show, God's glory is forthcoming and the schemes of the devil are destroyed. The armor of God reminds us who is worthy of praise and whose power is sufficient in the midst of our weaknesses. Unconditional truth is a byproduct of God's unconditional love and the Bible is God's love letter to us all.

#890 *"Those who are well pleased that there is a God, must be well pleased that there is a Bible."*

Always compare your circumstances with God's word. The Bible says if we believe the truth and abide by it, the truth will set us free, and who the Son sets free is free indeed.

"For His Glory" is a statement of faith that has everything to do with what

God has done to save and equip us to be transformed into His image. When the devil reminds you of your past let God's word do the talking. Do not ever settle for second-best in the kingdom. Jesus has chosen you and positioned you right now, at this moment, to be fruitful and to glorify God in your thoughts, words and deeds. "For His Glory" is not a thought well placed in our minds alone but a verbal proclamation that speaks to our soul that life is worth living and God is worthy of glory, honor and praise. This proclamation predetermines truth and a decision that says as John did, "He must increase and I must decrease". In Ephesians 1:11 the Bible says "also we have obtained an inheritance, having been predestined according to His purpose who works all things after the counsel of His will." Our lives have already been planned out, all we have to do is follow God's plan, saying amen to the counsel of His will that has been set forth before the beginning of time as we know it. Do not apologize for doing the right thing to a lost world based on being predestined by God. The question is are you taking on sainthood and answering the call of God for His glory? And why aren't the lost claiming their inheritance and blessings? The reason the world chooses self over Savior is because living in sin is more satisfying to them than living based on God's love, mercy and grace. Aren't we all good people and can't we all get along? When in reality, Jeremiah 17:9 says, "The heart is more deceitful than all else and is desperately sick…" The world and our flesh are more interested in unity than truth, acceptance and not holiness, the fear of man and not the reverence of God.

#917 *"You can declare and defend the truth, but unless you demonstrate it in your life it is of little value."*

Talk is cheap in the kingdom of God; the world is not interested in what you say or how you say it. Walking in the kingdom is walking in the power thereof, embracing the Spirit of God for His glory. How we demonstrate our relationship with Jesus will make all the difference in our world, and praise is our spiritual response that overrides negative reactions to circumstances. You never grow out of your relationship with Jesus, you grow into it. Our maturity has everything to do with God's glory, the manifestation of His presence in our lives. If God's presence is not visible in our day to day, our example is of little significance to the sphere of life around us. As we take on sainthood, we must not deny God's glory; a partial redemption was not given and our partial commitment is not enough.

God's glory is who God is, and if we do not live for His glory then we are not living who we are-children of God. Our adoption into the kingdom found in Galatians 4:4-7 tells us that we have inherited the Spirit of God, not as slaves with no free will, but sons and daughters with power to proclaim "Abba Father". Our eternal perspective should be twofold: us coming to God as Father but more important, our Father knowing us as sons and daughters through Christ. God cannot be more glorified in our lives than when He is proclaimed "Abba Father", an intimate proclamation of who God is and the position He holds in our lives. Nothing should take the place of our intimate relationship with the Father. Life circumstances pale in comparison to our walk with God, making tests testimonies and trials triumphs. To think that we have been chosen for glory through adoption should place an eternal gratitude that should change our earthly attitude. As Kings kids we have been given the full inheritance of divine blessings to obtain an abundant life and the responsibility to God's purpose and plan. But with every blessing from God comes our free will to embrace it. We will always be God's greatest challenge in our lives, because no matter what we have, love, power, truth, direction, etc., our willingness to accept the Father's plan either releases or limits Him in fulfilling it. When we accept God's plan we accept the process that will accomplish it. Believing in who God is and waiting on the Lord creates in us a better understanding of who we are and what our responsibilities look like.

#567 *"Before you can be a spokesman for Jesus, you must learn to sit quietly at His feet."*

The book of James tells us to be quick to listen and slow to speak. If we want to live our lives for God's glory we must train our minds to speak only when spoken to by the Lord. Any words that do not come from the heart of God and found in the book from God are probably soul driven and not Spirit led.

Before adoption we were restless souls searching for truth, dead in our sins, locked in an orphanage that provided us with no hope for our future and very little sustenance in our present. Starving for love, we sought every avenue of pleasure, seeking what we could not receive in the world, unconditional love. Wanting acceptance in sin we looked to false gods that only weakened our weakness, leaving us hopelessly in debt to a failed religion that functions on man's ability not God's availability. But when the glory of God was manifested in Jesus, the orphanage doors were open and a free invitation was given to all the lost souls of the earth to come and be part of His heavenly home where unconditional love was offered and despair was replaced with hope. The glory of God became the new norm of those who accepted this invitation. In the light of what was and what is, God's presence is necessary for us as a reminder of our adoption into the Father's forever family. "For His Glory" should be on our minds and in our hearts every waking moment of our day, reflecting our love and appreciation for "Abba Father".

#578 *"Add this to your daily prayer, this I know, that God is for me."*

It is critical for us to understand that God's spiritual blessing and power overrule all circumstantial experiences in life. That is why we can have peace in the midst of conflict, joy in pain and love in fear. The mystery of God's plan takes us to places where physical challenges may confront us, but cannot overwhelm us because we have been given the spiritual power to be over-comers in Christ. Remember: Faith is the assurance of things hoped for, the conviction of things not seen. If we as children of God can embrace such a lifestyle and not be distracted by temporal conditions in life, we will not be shaken by the attack against our soul to react and flee from the truth of God's promises for our welfare. David writes in Psalm 56:9-11 when seized by the Philistines in Gath "...This I know, that God is for me. In God, whose word I praise, In the Lord, whose word I praise, In God I have put my trust, I shall not be afraid..." "This I know, that God is for me" says to all hindrances in life's journey, I may not understand what is going on or why it is necessary, but my trust is in the Lord, who knew me while I was yet in my mother's womb, and predestined me to adoption before the foundation of this earth was even formed. I will not be overcome by doubt, distracted by what I see, or deceived by what I don't understand. My faith is in God's love for me and that He will never leave me or forsake me in my journey to fulfill His purpose and plan. Sooner or later every Christian will realize that living for Jesus is a battleground, not a playground and holiness is a lifestyle not an afterthought. The joy of the battleground is complete victory, the battle belongs to the Lord and the Lord never loses. Our partnership in the battle is believing and committing to the Father's war plan. Too often what happens is laziness causes us to become complacent, we start to live on yesterday's victories and our daily preparation for battle is less about putting on the Lord Jesus Christ, making no provision for the flesh and meditating on God's current word and more about putting off prayer and praise, turning hope into wishful thinking instead of part of our arsenal of worship.

#625 "Human nature will always limit Jesus to man's perspective."

When we live "For His Glory" it is the otherness of Jesus that is brought to the forefront of our eternal perspective. Our human nature is our greatest challenge in worship because it sees life from earth up instead of heaven down. We must live life based on what God has brought us through the life, death and resurrection of Jesus Christ. Our human nature will always find credit for something that only God can provide, that is why so much emphasis is placed on the fact that being good is enough to reject God being God. If the world believed that Jesus was God, it would repent for being good. Being good is never enough, that is why Jesus came to solve our human nature problem and provide us with His otherness-holiness that cannot be duplicated from earth up. We are lost in our human religion if we don't surrender to the otherness of Jesus. You have heard it said to think out of the box, God's word says think out of this world. Everything pertaining to life and godliness has nothing to do with our human nature or our worldview but instead the Spiritual nature given to us through Christ.

Chapter Eight
Taking Ownership

When Jesus came from heaven in fulfillment of God's redemption plan, He had already taken ownership of His role in our forgiveness and healing. His total commitment to our salvation made it possible for Him to refer back to that moment in time when He took His first breath of earth's atmosphere and on a regular basis throughout His life, remembering who He was in fulfilling God's purpose and plan for our lives. To own something is to take responsibility for it. In Christ's case, He took responsibility as our savior and lived His life to fulfill that calling. When tempted in the wilderness, He exampled the use of God's word to defeat the devil, always relying on the truth to expose the lies or half-truths of deception. If it is not ours we do not fight for it; that is human nature. How much more should we own our salvation and fight the good fight of faith in believing the Father's love, mercy and grace is sufficient and that in our weakness His strength is perfected. Jesus owned our salvation throughout the most difficult times of His life, choosing the cross over His will be done. The Garden of Gethsemane was that moment in time when emotions ran high, His death loomed near and the test of His ownership was in full display. Jesus prayed to the Father, My soul is burdened, if it is possible, remove this cup of My blood offering from Me; yet not My will, but Yours be done.

#230 *"Growing in love with Jesus is the key to overcoming the soul of man."*

When the Father in His great love for us said no to His Son, He said yes to us. It was at that moment ownership was being transferred in the heavenlies.

Jesus committed to pay the price for our sins; the documents for forgiveness and adoption were signed by the blood of the Messiah. A new law was given, one of love, mercy and grace. The debt was paid in full and God's redemption from heaven down was complete and validated on the day of Christ's resurrection. Man's greatest fear, death, was defeated, eternal life was proven true and an invitation was given to all. If you believe in My Son you will have life, good days and bad days will turn into God days, love will cast out fear and you will be given willpower and the freedom to choose joy instead of sadness, hope instead of despair, peace in the midst of conflict and trust in place of doubt. If you think about it, it is amazing that God in Christ gave up His deity, suffered the legal penalty of sin and died just to give us the freedom to choose. Through it all Jesus did not secure justification, redemption and sanctification for us, only the freedom to choose it. That is unconditional love that cannot be found in this world. No one in this world would give up so much without something in return. Romans 5:8 says, "But God demonstrates His own love towards us, in that while we were yet sinners, Christ died for us." There will never be another man like Jesus and as we take on sainthood let's remember the example set before us in regard to selfless love. Taking ownership of our Christianity involves several steps of maturity. As we examine some of these steps let us never leave unconditional love; it is God's foundation by which we choose to live. Redemption was initiated with God's love in Bethlehem, tested in Gethsemane, finished on Calvary and validated on Resurrection Sunday. This is the pattern by which we live. Everything we think, say and do shall be done with unconditional love. The continuance of God's love is found in our willingness to do God's will no matter how much our souls may object. Perseverance through this lifestyle until the end will validate our resurrected love for Jesus. Matthew 24:13 says, "But the one who endures to the end, he will be saved". Unconditional love produces unconditional trust and just as Jesus gave His all for our freedom to choose, we must give our all and believe that Jesus is the way, truth and life.

TAKING ON SAINTHOOD

#695 "Legitimate desires and illegitimate demands are a thin line we must never cross; to cross it is to erode our faith and to submit to reasonable feelings."

Taking ownership takes on many different causes throughout our journey with Christ. As we look at some of these causes let's remember that our faith in Christ releases God's love, mercy and grace; we are saved by grace through faith. So as we take ownership in life, do it with a desire for God's spiritual blessings and do not allow soul driven demands in Jesus name dictate how you perceive life. There is, to a great degree, very little "reasonable" in God's word, the mysteries of God is what faith is all about. What we as Christians have in common is faith, not answered prayer. God gives what He wants, to who He wants, when He wants to. That does not mean He loves one more than the other, but it does mean that God is sovereign and He knows what is best for us who believe. James 1:2-4 says, "Consider it all joy, my brethren, when you encounter various trials, knowing that the testing of your faith produces endurance. And let endurance have its perfect result, so that you may be perfect and complete, lacking in nothing." The process of maturing involves trials; opportunities to develop and build on the foundation of being a child of God. If we do not lead with joy daily and view life and not seasons in life worthy of praise, we will trend down to trying to make sense of God's purpose, instead of thanking Him for His presence in the midst of storms. When God says no, He has a perfect reason for His choice; our faith and trust in God will cause us to worship and not worry, rejoice and not rebel and give thanks instead of making illegitimate demands based on the down side of heaven looking up. If your tendencies in life are to have mood swings based on your feelings and circumstances, you are living a soul driven life. Happiness concerns you more than rejoicing and trusting in God's promises that develop you spiritually. Remember: Joy is a choice to rejoice.

Happiness depends on happenings in which we may have no control.

#699 *"Our human tendencies are to be relieved of our pain in the midst of trials instead of being motivated to rejoice in God's sovereignty."*

The Holy Spirit brings us to our first step in ownership, that is owning the fact that we have sinned and fallen short of the glory of God. The wages of sin is death, but we have a free gift from God, eternal life in Christ. Unconditional love involves giving and forgiving. When we accept Jesus and repent of our sins, God forgives us and cleanses us from all unrighteousness. Taking ownership of our sins comes with no excuses; no the devil did not make you do it although he may have given you options and you were foolish enough to pursue them. It was not your parents fault; we are all born sinners. No one is responsible for your sin but you. This is very important, because if you do not take ownership of your failed life you will enter your new born again life in Christ blaming others and circumstances for your problems instead of being responsible to God. True sorrow precedes joy. I believe joy is a part of repentance that is necessary to experience Christ. A forgiving heart is filled with joy and a spiritual sense of being loved. When someone pays a debt, the recipient of forgiveness is overjoyed by the relief of that burden. If our repentance is not one with God but instead involves the faults of others, our Christianity will be flawed and easily deceived. Our tendencies will be to excuse our future sins based on people and circumstances. If you have trouble experiencing joy, it might just be that you have not truly experienced sorrow. Sorrow and joy are choices that must be made in order to embrace the fullness of God in our day to day.

TAKING ON SAINTHOOD

#132 *"Don't look back unless it is in reminiscence of God's faithfulness to bring hope for the moment."*

Taking ownership of God's word is a step in a righteous direction. As a child of God letting God's word define who you are is vital to your maturity. The key to discipleship is truth and Jesus said I am the way the truth and the life; no one comes to the Father but through Me and we will know the truth and the truth will set us free. In John 17:17 Jesus prays this to the Father on our behalf, "Sanctify them in the truth; Your word is truth." David writes in Psalm 119:11 "Your word I have treasured in my heart, that I may not sin against You."

Two things are important when owning Scripture. God's word is true, God cannot lie and it sets us apart for God's service. The first sin in the garden of Eden was a soul driven choice based on a half-truth spoken as a complete truth resulting in a lie. If we study to show ourselves approved we will not be deceived by the half-truths of the enemy in our day to day and our choices will be Spirit led not soul driven. Our flesh, the world and the devil will always question the truth of God's word using our trials to question it's validity and whether or not God even loves us. Our sanctification is based on truth and our service to others on us being holy, set apart for God's service. Owning the word means having faith in it, believing it to be true and not allowing anything to hinder that belief system. I Peter 5:6-7 says, "Therefore humble yourselves under the mighty hand of God, that He may exalt you at the proper time, casting all your anxiety on Him, because He cares for you."

The world places unity above truth, it proclaims all religions lead to the same God, being good based on your own perspective is good enough and there is no final judgment. The world's unity goes against everything found in God's word; it has nothing to do with holiness and truth, only the lies of the enemy repeated from Eden.

Remember: Walking with Jesus is a spiritual journey; we must draw our identity and strength from the scripture. Knowing who we are is vital in fulfilling what God called us to be. Walking in the Spirit allows us to engage with confidence the lessons we must learn in the school of Christ. Keep it spiritual and you will keep it eternal. The temporal is but a moment and you must seize the moment, looking to Christ, or the moment will seize you and feelings will dictate your reaction to life's circumstances-not faith in believing.

#1025 *"Nothing around us is as important as He who is in us."*

When God's word refers to us as more than conquerors it has little to do with the physical atmosphere around us and all to do with the power of God within us. Knowing that we have been given, through His divine power, everything pertaining to life in the Spirit and a focus towards God, we can choose to summon the power of God to overcome our soul driven reactions and instead release the character of God's love, joy, peace, patience, kindness, goodness, faithfulness, gentleness and self-control to turn every trial and temptation into triumphs. If we could look upon our difficulties as an opportunity to embrace the sufficiency of God's grace, it would allow us to preserve our souls and to glorify Jesus. The enemy will attempt to change our names throughout our journey, names like fearful, anxious, angry, unforgiving, hopeless, bitter, unfulfilled, lonely, insignificant, victim, unhappy, etc. Every one of these ungodly names involves temporal circumstances in the midst of God's eternal plan. If you focus on sight and what seems to be, you limit your faith and hope. When you find yourself in a holding pattern, it is usually the Lord waiting for you to catch up to His purpose and plan.

There is no downtime in the kingdom of God only uplifting promises that, when yoked with Jesus, turn burdens into opportunities for God to work in our lives.

#248 "A victorious Christian turns every trying experience into a means to glorify God."

What is so important about God's word is that it must be studied and applied. Like everything found in the kingdom, application in life is the key that unlocks the mysteries of Jesus. How did Jesus do what He did? He had faith in the Father and was the living Word of God. Jesus took on every temptation known to man and was more than a conqueror through them because He took ownership of His heavenly calling seriously and believed the Father through it all. God's word, when lived, causes us to rejoice always, pray without ceasing and in everything give thanks, for that is the will of God concerning us.

Another cause in life that is worth taking ownership of is the call to witness. God's word is based on two principles-wholeness and witness. Everywhere in scripture one of these two principles are taught. Wholeness is being all that God has called us to be and witness shows others how to accomplish wholeness. Words like lights in the world, ambassadors and disciples are used to describe those that are whole through God's redeeming grace and live as witnesses of His redemption. It is never enough to become whole in Christ, being a witness of redemption is all part of the wholeness plan. If you truly embrace salvation as you should, a free gift from God for the forgiveness of your sins, you will do everything in His power to example and share this good news as well. When we take on sainthood we take on the ownership of witness to the sphere of life around us. Knowing the truth and hiding it under a bushel does not fulfill God's redemption plan in your life. If we are not taking advantage of teachable moments in life to share

God's love, we are hoarding what God has called us to give away. Jesus tells His disciples in Matthew 10:27, "What I tell you in the darkness, speak in the light; and what you hear whispered in your ear, proclaim upon the housetops." Exampling the love of Jesus starts with a lifestyle and translates into conversation. I believe there is an accountability factor found in witnessing that helps us to walk the straight and narrow. If no one knows you are a Christian it's easier to bend your values and not stay true to God's call in your life. Positive, personal peer pressure helps us to seek after God more fully so that we have an answer to those who desire forgiveness and healing in Jesus. So often we are the only examples of Jesus the lost see and that is why wholeness and witness go hand in hand throughout the Bible.

#612 *"Evangelism reveals the Savior, discipleship reveals the Lord."*

The good news of the gospel is a public service announcement, serving others is an automatic overflow of a personal relationship with Jesus. Discipling is another important way we can take ownership of witnessing. Our witness can teach other believers the values and priorities of scripture. We will disciple someone, someway, somehow, at some time, throughout our lives. When we witness to Christians we encourage them to stay the course and not give up fighting the good fight of faith. To witness is to teach and in doing so we follow in the footsteps of Jesus. Paul said it well, "Follow me as I follow Jesus". The challenge for Paul was to follow Jesus, his challenge to others was to do the same. Witness has much to do with what is caught as well as taught. If our actions do not validate our words our witness is in vain. The sphere of life around us is steeped with words that have little value from an eternal perspective. When Jesus came He did away with worldly ways and words that produce dead works, instead He fulfilled God's purpose and plan and spoke life into a dying world, filled with dishonor, prejudice and dysfunction.

#22 "We should always take pleasure in our trials so as to be ready to give an account of God's love, mercy and grace."

Taking on sainthood is taking ownership of God's love, mercy and grace through a lifestyle of godly words and works of truth reflecting the heart of the Father in Christ.

TAKING ON SAINTHOOD

Chapter Nine

Caring For The Lost

As we take on sainthood, caring for the lost is one of the more difficult challenges in Christianity. It sounds simple but involves a disciplined soul that must not lose touch with God's plan for salvation and the unconditional love that initiated its beginning. This is one area of our Christianity where our prayer life is seriously lacking. In our day to day we will come across many of those who, for some reason or another, have chosen to ignore or flat out reject the gospel of salvation. This I believe is where praying without ceasing comes into play. The lost, in so many ways, cannot defend themselves or choose not to. They enjoy being slaves to the gods of this world including self. But this does not change the fact that God called us to defend them with truth, even if it is from a distance and communication on their behalf is between us and God, not them. It is always better if the gospel is shared but if not, praying in the Spirit on their behalf is necessary. Caring for the lost is actually fulfilling the purpose of redemption in our lives. We must learn to live saved and never forget the two-fold purpose of our salvation: to become a light and be a light for a lost world darkened with sin. So just as God's love motivated His plan for redemption, our love in Christ should empower and instruct us to love enough to pray for the redeemed and those who are not redeemed yet. The power of prayer is instrumental in redemption, Jesus prayed for us even before we existed. Prayer and the scripture are our offensive weapons of God against the schemes of the enemy.

#203 "Too often we pray to man before we pray to God."

Ephesians 6:18 tells us, "With all prayer and petition pray at all times in the Spirit, and with this in view, be on the alert with all perseverance and petition for all the saints." In Luke 19:10 the Scripture says, "For the Son of Man has come to seek and save that which was lost." And In Acts 26:17-18, Paul shares Jesus commission to him, "...to whom I am sending you, to open their eyes so that they may turn from darkness to light and from the dominion of Satan to God, that they may receive forgiveness of sins and an inheritance among those who have been sanctified by faith in Me." The word tells us to pray for slaves and saints that they will experience God's best in their life. We do not know the inner workings of the Spirit in the sphere of life around us, but this we do know, that God has compassion for all and His love does not hinge on what others do, only on what Jesus has done. If we lack compassion we will be less likely to care much about the lost and their future and our prayer life would do little in battle against the enemy in regard to their souls. Care proceeds prayer, if we are not praying for the lost we do not really care much about their need for Jesus and their eternal damnation. You must be convinced that Jesus wants all of you and wants you to give others all of Him.

Remember: We all play an important role in redemption. Jesus did not come into the world isolated from need, just the opposite, He came as a vulnerable baby dependent on others to catch the vision of redemption and doing their part in seeing it succeed. So view the lost as babies dependent on us to defend them and their struggles, to see through their darkness into His glorious light, and from the power of Satan unto God that they may be sanctified by faith in Jesus.

#783 *"Love is what makes us valuable."*

If God's love initiates the plan of redemption, then His love should initiate our caring for the lost. Let's not try to figure out the lost around us, let's just love them unconditionally and do what we can to share God's redemption in our lives. Unconditional love does not depend on how others react to us, but our response to God. We must find a way in our hearts to love the lost and to take advantage of teachable moments to share the love that Jesus has for us. Our value is based on God's love, do not forget how God used others to lead us to Jesus and receive Him as Savior and Lord. I believe we are all called to reflect the love of God in our lives without shame or excuse, and in doing so, we worship Him and witness His saving grace to whoever is ready to do the same. The fullness of God is found in His love.

Caring for the lost needs to start somewhere; we all need to find where that somewhere is and plant a seed of that commitment to love. The easiest way is to love without prejudice. This does not mean as the world says "love is love" or to ignore sinful behavior. There is no true love in the world without God. Our sacrifice to love is based on our response to Jesus response to us- unconditional. Keeping holiness before us at all times does not define love as acceptance but instead as extraordinary. Just as Jesus loved us in spite of our sin, we get to love the lost in spite of theirs. Remember: The world wants unity with God without submitting to God's plan of redemption producing unity. There is no unity without truth, that is why Jesus brought division to this world. He made love available without compromise, the purpose of redemption, that is to provide salvation to the lost through one way, one truth and one life. His purity precedes power and we can only become children of God through purity, repentance and the forgiveness of sin. Caring for the lost does not mean we compromise the truth of God's word. The whole concept of caring needs to start with the gospel of Jesus; it clarifies truth and unity; it is why we do what we do as unto the Lord.

TAKING ON SAINTHOOD

#771 *"Our emotions should always be tempered with holiness."*

Jude 1:20–23 says, "But you, beloved, building yourselves up on your most holy faith, praying in the Holy Spirit, keep yourselves in the love of God, waiting anxiously for the mercy of our Lord Jesus Christ to eternal life. And have mercy on some, who are doubting; save others, snatching them out of the fire; and on some have mercy with fear, hating even the garment polluted by the flesh." It seems very clear that once we begin our journey as children of God and taking on sainthood we are to be Spirit led and no longer soul driven. Disciplining our soul to stay within the limits of holiness allows us to act on the revelation of God's word and not the feelings of man or the opinions of the world. Caring for the lost is a spiritual command from God's word; go to all nations preaching the gospel, baptizing them in the name of the Father, the Son and the Holy Spirit. Everything done in caring for the lost begins with the Gospel of Jesus. The gospel should be what draws you to care and the main focus as to why you care. Even the dollars you give the homeless on the street corner says "In God we trust". One of the few times anxious is used in a positive way is here, waiting anxiously for the mercy of our Lord Jesus Christ to eternal life. God's mercy on our behalf must be transferred to the lost who doubt the existence of God. Our acts of mercy will do one of three things: plant a seed of hope, water a seed of hope or harvest the fruit of hope. It does not matter what part our mercy plays in the heart of a lost soul as long as hope is presented. Our mercy will partner with God's mercy when our obedience rules over our fear.

TAKING ON SAINTHOOD

#888 "The greatest temptation in life is fear, thus lowering the standard of faith."

God's word tells us that He has not given to us a spirit of fear, but love, power and a disciplined mind. Our walk with Jesus should reflect these three qualities: love, power and a disciplined mind. A disciplined mind holds every thought captive in obedience to Christ, dwells on the power of God not the frailty of man and loves unconditionally. Fear is the enemy's greatest tool to tempt us from fulfilling God's purpose and plan. Selflessness disarms the enemies attack. When Savior replaces self, demons flee and the power of love conquers the spirit of fear. If we could only remember that our caring for the lost is a simple act of kindness and obedience, and when we love without prejudice, knowing that God is the one who saves, heals, restores and provides, the spirit of fear has no power. Planting, watering and harvesting in mercy is all we can do. It is God who causes the growth and only God knows the heart of the lost we serve and His timing for salvation is not our time or responsibility. God truly makes it easy for both salvation and caring for the lost possible. All it takes is an obedient, willing heart set on wanting God's best for a world that is living their worst of times. Let your faith rule your actions and your words as you take on sainthood knowing that God has a plan even when you do not see the results of your obedience to care for the lost.

Chapter Ten

Having the Mind of Christ

There is much we do not know about the mind of man, things that provoke it and its strong connection with our soul. We do the things we shouldn't do and don't do the things that we should. We are easily fractured and hold contempt, forgetting good things and harboring past transgressions. The mind of man sees through the eyes of the flesh and is quick to react to circumstances. It's thoughts are hard to harness and teaching it to do what is right in the eyes of God is not possible in its natural state. Until we accept the fact that our minds are disruptive and must be renewed, we will fail miserably. Having the mind of Christ is not training the old, but giving birth to the new. The mind of Christ does not get caught up in what is seen or seems to be but instead what is known through God's word. Everything in life starts with a thought and it is the thought that the enemy uses to tempt and deceive us. A spiritually renewed mind is necessary to walk a Spirit-filled life.

#376 "Rejoice in what you know."

The renewal of the mind always changes the way we think and even more important a renewed mind gives us the power to think for God's glory. Too often we get caught up in behavior and focus on that aspect of life, when in reality our focus should always be on our minds, the author of our actions. The question is not so much "What Would Jesus Do?" as much as "What Would Jesus Think?" The mind of Christ is directly connected to the heart of God. It is not easily fractured, does not hold grudges and constantly reminisces on the remedies of God's word, producing holy behavior. The mind of Christ does not need to be taught, instead it teaches us. When we become Christians old things pass away and new things take their place, our old mind is transplanted with the mind of Christ. How does that work? I am not sure, but this I know, when I deepen my knowledge of God I think spiritual thoughts and I make spiritual choices. The mystery is in Christ; He holds the key, His life, death and resurrection has given to us the power to become and the mainstay of becoming is His mind. Transformation takes place when we renew our minds with the truth of God's word and are led by God's Spirit. Having the mind of Christ is a choice we make and is necessary for embracing holiness. The mind of Christ holds every thought captive, destroys vain imagination, dwells on what is known and not seen, and gives glory to the Father. There are no pity parties in Christ, only a deep contentment and knowledge that He lives and that He lives in us.

#728 *"Whenever faith is ruled by our eyes we lose sight of God at work and only see the limitations of the temporal."*

The mind of Christ distinguishes the things of God given to us by God. When we begin to think like Jesus we make choices reflecting God's will be done; God's glory our priority and understanding that not understanding is part of the mystery of Christ. In the natural none of this is possible, but he who is spiritual judges all things and in Christ this judgment leading to holiness is acceptable in the eyes of God. Having the mind of Christ creates in us a singular mindset that refuses to accept half-truths and opinions as valid subject matter in regard to making choices with God's glory in the balance. Double-mindedness is birthed in doubt and questions God's character and His love for His children. James 1:5-8 says, "But if any of you lacks wisdom, let him ask of God, who gives to all generously and without reproach, and it will be given to him. But he must ask in faith without any doubting, for the one who doubts is like the surf of the sea, driven and tossed by the wind. For that man ought not to expect that he will receive anything from the Lord, being a double-minded man, unstable in all his ways." Double- mindedness should not be taken lightly, it is not a term we Christians want to be labeled with or in any way associated with as part of our day to day. Taking on sainthood is protecting and preserving the mind of Christ within us no matter what is going on around us. The mind of Christ eliminates divisive thoughts and is not interested if God does not receive the glory. The schemes of the devil draw our attention away from God's purpose and tries to pique our interest in someone or thing that has no relevance to who God is.

#315 *"Every circumstance that creates an emotion is a God-given opportunity to glorify Jesus."*

Disciplining our soul to be one with Christ allows the mind of Christ to grow in it's thought vocabulary. Words like honor, truth, character, purity, righteousness, holiness, become the mainstay that draw our attention instead of words like doubt, anger, anxiety, and fear. We still have to take ownership of Christ-likeness in order for us to rejoice in trials or temptations, making choices based on God's interest and not our own. We must stand on holy ground. If our life is divided and we stand in two places having two minds we fall into the trap of compromise. There is only one way, truth, and life, no one gets to the Father any other way but through Jesus. Faith again is the mainstay in the renewal of our minds. We must be assured that God is present when thought provoking circumstances challenge our faith and question God's word, the truth that secures our soul. Taking on sainthood requires standing in the kingdom for the kingdom, you cannot split your allegiance. Jesus said you're either for Me or against Me. Our minds, renewed by the truth of God's word, keep us safe within the borders of the kingdom of God. The mind of Christ chooses to think in a godly manner and contentment is the supernatural overflow into the soul of man. I Peter 1:13-16 tells us, "Therefore, prepare your minds for action, keep sober in spirit, fix your hope completely on the grace to be brought to you at the revelation of Jesus Christ. As obedient children, do not be conformed to the former lusts which were yours in your ignorance, but like the Holy One who called you, be holy yourselves also in all your behavior; because it is written, "YOU SHALL BE HOLY, FOR I AM HOLY."

The mind of Christ prepares for action, if you are standing still you're falling behind. Jesus never stopped moving ahead for the glory set before Him, even in His prayer life He was advancing the kingdom of God. His peace was His Father's presence actively engaged with His purpose and plan.

#810 "Our eyes will never be satisfied until we see Him, our hearts will never be content until we know Him and our lives will never be fulfilled until we serve Him."

Jesus tells us if you come to Me, listen to Me and act on what you hear you will build your life on a solid foundation and the storms of life will not destroy who you are. Not so for the man who comes and hears but refuses to act upon what he hears. This man's destruction will be great. (Matthew 7:24–27) Storms are inevitable, misery is optional. We get to believe and become or disbelieve and allow renegade thoughts to hinder the mind of Christ and create a makeshift Christianity where our "soul" purpose in life becomes more important than God's will be done. So how do we prepare the mind for action? Hebrews 4 tells us that the word of God judges the thoughts and intentions of the heart.

Once again, I do not quite understand how the heart and mind are connected, but scripture clearly shows us they are; it is part of the mystery of Christ. A pure heart defines the parameters of the mind transforming it to think as Jesus thought, creating the mind of Christ. Transformation starts with a born-again spirit. The Spirit child desires God's best and joyfully anticipates God's purpose and plan, holding every thought captive in obedience to Christ. I believe God's Spirit in us, through a knowledge of God's word, develops a standard of holiness that the mind uses to separate good and evil within our thought patterns.

#950 *"Wake up every morning with Jesus in your heart and God's plan for living on your mind."*

God's word teaches us how to walk in the Spirit and not carry out the desires of the flesh, to minimize our thoughts in order to maximize our potential. Remember: The devil does not want the simplicity of the gospel to be our mindset but instead, the complexity of life as the world knows it. The mind of Christ eliminates drama and pursues a divine perspective limiting our thoughts to God's purpose and plan.

Jesus gives us a unique description of the mind of Christ in John 5:30, "I can do nothing on My own initiative. As I hear, I judge; and My judgment is just, because I do not seek My own will, but the will of Him who sent Me." The mind of Christ hears and judges based on the will of the Father. Jesus was dependent on the Father, He judged with righteous intent. Only when we are independently dependent on Jesus will our thoughts translate to righteous intentions, reflected in our words and actions. There is a strong correlation between hearing and thinking; when we hear the word of God our minds are stimulated with spiritual options in which choices must be made. As a Christian, when God speaks to me in my spirit, my mind is involved and choices are the next step in fulfilling God's will. Remember: hearing alone is not enough, we must act in faith in order to be overcomers, our thoughts dictate our actions in the storms of life.

#597 *"Know your hope for eternity and your purpose for the present."*

When Jesus says, "I can do nothing on my own initiative, as I hear I judge", He is setting a standard of dependence that glorifies the Father within the framework of His mind. Only when we realize that we are bankrupt morally and spiritually will we embrace the mind of Christ. Matthew 5:3 tells us, "Blessed are the poor in spirit, for theirs is the kingdom of heaven." Our maturity has nothing to do with moving on but instead, building upon. This is key to growth, we can do nothing on our own, as we hear we judge, we dwell not on our own will but the will of Him who saves us. Our hearing should be thought-provoking and the choices we make in that moment will reflect the mind of Christ or the self-righteous mind of man. It is better to rejoice first than to repent quickly. How do we possess the mind of Christ and not relinquish its power in our lives? Philippians 4:8 tells us that the way to renew the mind and possess a divine perspective is to dwell on truth, honor, righteousness, purity, loveliness, good repute, excellence and anything praiseworthy. When our minds are filled with these qualities of life, we will have little room for negative, worldly, self- serving thoughts. Here is the answer to the question-take control of your thoughts by allowing the Holy Spirit to fill your mind. The mind of Christ is holy ground and it should be treated with reverence and worship. It truly is a mystery within our being but not an unreachable, impossible part of God's redeeming us body, soul, spirit, mind and strength. Just believe throughout your day to day and God will provide the mind of Christ. It is necessary for taking on sainthood and building upon our position as a child of God.

#767 *"Without obedience there is no sacrifice."*

Our confidence in knowing Jesus plays an important part of the mind of Christ. When Jesus says My judgment is just, because I obey the Father's will and not My own, we take on that same confidence in our obedience to God. Our obedience starts with believing what God has called us to become. When we know the truth that sets us free, we have fulfilled the importance of abiding in the word, establishing faith based on facts. Holiness is embraced when we are quick to listen, slow to speak and slow to anger; for man's anger in any form does not achieve the righteousness of God. When we make choices, "As I hear I judge," in unity with the Holy Spirit, we lead with joy, knowing that just as God is so will we be.

TAKING ON SAINTHOOD

Chapter Eleven

Intentional

Living out our constant Christianity involves godly intent on our behalf, waking up every morning determined to know nothing except Jesus Christ and Him crucified for the glory of God. To live intentional is to live with purpose in accomplishing God's plan for today. Paul tells us in Ephesians 5:1, "Therefore be imitators of God, as beloved children." Mimicking God is a good way to start your day: Jesus prayed, so pray; Jesus spoke the truth in love, so speak the truth in love; Jesus forgave, so forgive; God loved and gave, so love and give. Spiritual stability is key to intentional living, it is the basis of who we are and how we live. If we are not walking in the Spirit, we are carrying out the desires of the flesh. Our *God intentions* will keep us on the straight and narrow where Jesus walks.

#391 "Distance, distraction, disbelief and disobedience hinder our hearing the voice of God."

Hearing the voice of God is not just a good idea, it is necessary for development and overall health and well-being. It is not above God to shout on behalf of our deliverance, but He would prefer to whisper. His shouts of deliverance only come when we have deliberately distanced ourselves from Him and the distractions of that distance drown out His guiding whispers. Just think of how awesome it would be if we deliberately choose to stay close to His presence and obey His every whisper; peace that surpasses understanding would cause us to stay the course and joy would be our strength in the midst of trials. An intentional walk with Jesus does not just happen, it takes a willingness to decrease so that the power of God may increase. John the Baptist was willing to decrease so that Christ may increase, not only in his own life but also the lives of others. When John saw Jesus, he saw the Lamb of God who takes away the sins of the world, that perspective determined his decrease. We could learn much from John the Baptist, he was referred to by Jesus as the greatest man to walk the earth, quite a compliment from the King of kings and Lord of lords. So what made John so great? It was not his position in this world, he was a lowly itinerant preacher that had a limited message, "Repent and be baptized". It was not his stately attire; camel skin was not the affluent dress of his time. Nor was it his appearance that made him great. His greatness came in knowing that Jesus was the Lamb of God who took away the sins of the world and through that knowledge he declined recognition in this world, lifting up Jesus in his place. What would our sainthood look like if we lifted up Jesus in our place? Our sainthood would look humble yet confident, fragile yet strong, limited in vocabulary yet powerful in wisdom, not distracted by the powers that be but delivered through the Holy Spirit of God within us. If you want to have greatness and power in your sainthood you must possess and protect simplicity in your child like faith.

#347 "Whatever we focus on we reinforce."

If our focus is on the temporal we will seek solutions that only bring us temporal satisfaction and the power of God is limited because of our soul driven choices. There is nothing wrong with wanting sickness to leave, relationships to be healed, finances to be improved and family to be restored. But if we lose our eternal perspective and stop standing on the promises of God in the midst of the storms, we will sink into a depressed state of mind. It is not a problem to ask God questions, but it is a problem to question God's answers. Questioning God's timing is a slippery slope that never leads to victory. If we minimize our focus we will maximize our perspective, keep your eyes on Jesus; one of the devils most effective tools is distraction. If he can get you to look elsewhere, half of the battle is won. An eternal perspective focuses on Jesus, allowing us to see beyond the now and opens up for us God's plan that goes beyond our limitations of sight, entering the war zone of faith. If you want to please God, believe that He is and that He is a rewarder of those who seek Him. (Hebrews 11:6)

#362 "Eternal choices, develops eternal priorities, producing eternal rewards."

If you are standing still you are falling behind. Reinforcements are necessary if you plan and prepare to live intentionally. God's word is a great example of eternity; it provides us with God's point of view. If we truly believe that God has spoken, we will make every effort to prioritize God's love, mercy and grace in the midst of temporal circumstances. If Jesus saw beyond the cross we must see from the cross. That is where healing truly takes place, not the removal of developmental trials but the joy of His presence providing us with the eternal rewards that can only be seen from Calvary. A pure heart sees God and if it does not see God it looks elsewhere. Focusing on eternity in the temporal world is never ending, the choices we make based on God's purpose and plan help us to prioritize what is necessary in our day to day. So when we choose to study God's word, that choice puts us in a position to allow God's word to study our motives and correct our soul driven tendencies, developing our priorities as God is, not as what seems to be.

Being chosen and having the power to choose should be what we give thanks for in everything. We cannot be overwhelmed by circumstances if we choose to stand fast in the liberty knowing Christ has set us free and choose not to be entangled again with the yoke of bondage. The yoke of bondage is a perspective we choose, a temporal perspective feeding our emotions, limiting our trust in God's eternal purpose. This does not mean we ignore life in real time, it simply means that life in real time is not the conclusion of our story, only a small sample of God's on-going deliverance based on His eternal plan. When we prioritize life based on God's promises and not man's problems we see God at work even when our vision is shaded by circumstances. If you want to learn more about your priorities in life, keep a journal of what you say over a period of a month, that will give you a good idea of what you believe.

#343 *"Let's live each day in Christ; I did instead of I should've, I will instead of I would've and I can instead of I could've."*

As we take on sainthood, *God intentions* should be our priority. Our godly intentions to know the truth daily gives us the manna for the day, bringing contentment and knowing that God is in control no matter what seems out of control because we have searched God's word and we trust God's character. And just like manna, it is only good for today. We cannot live on yesterday's victories; every day brings us new challenges and our daily devotion to God's word meets those challenges in real time. If you catch yourself saying I should've known better, what you are really confessing is that you did not give God's word the opportunity to prepare you for today's lesson. Psalms 18:3 says, "I call upon the Lord, who is worthy to be praised, and I am saved from my enemies." Our prayer life reflects worship to God because it intentionally acknowledges God's omnipotence, omniscience and omnipresence. When we start each day with prayer choosing to call upon the Lord, our confession will not be, "I should've prayed," but instead "I will trust Him today because I met with Him this morning and my faith is full." And when your faith is full you can do all things through Christ who strengthens you. (Philippians 4:13)

When we come to Jesus we die to the old patterns of life and take on His new ones. Our old patterns come naturally; they became who we are over our years of self-serving worship. The new creation patterns are not naturally developed, but supernaturally experienced. Choices, priorities, perspectives and God-like intentions create our daily walk with Christ. The patterns that we choose to create in the Spirit and the priorities we develop in knowing the truth, reward us with victory in our day to day. Planned spontaneity is key to surrender and obedience. Spiritual gain does not just happen based on what Jesus did, but instead our response to what Jesus did in humble surrender.

#381 *"Pause, pray, praise, ponder and proceed."*

We intentionally pray, praise and study to show ourselves approved, but for some self- righteous reason we get caught off guard and stumble, reacting to life's challenges instead of responding to God's presence in awe and wonder. There is a reason God's word uses terms like *always, nothing, without ceasing* and *in everything*. When we pray in the morning, before our day begins, we are reminded that Jesus is alive, He is available and His Holy Spirit will lead us throughout our day to day. The love of the Father will keep us safe and there is no fear in His love. Our morning conversations with God should have little to do with our wants and more to do with developing a relationship with our Savior. When unconditional love is acknowledged and received, unconditional trust is established. But emotions run high in the human soul and need to be led by the Spirit. When we do not pause throughout the day to converse with God, focusing on His presence, promises and power, we slip into soul driven mode, feelings take over and self wants back on the throne. The pause that refreshes is an important part of constant Christianity, reminding us that God is God and we are His children, who are anxious for nothing but instead are unconditionally trusting His unconditional love.

Scripture says much about repentance; we think a high standard in Christ is being quick to repent, but in reality it is a low standard of humanity. God has shown us a more productive way. Instead of being quick to repent, be first to rejoice. That is the pause that maintains our eternal perspective and victory throughout our day to day. If we remember that Jesus loves us and we love Jesus, we will better understand God's purpose and plan at any given moment. Understanding God's love produces composure under pressure. Everything God does is intentional for our well-being. God sets the example of intent, that is why the Bible tells us to give thanks in everything. God is love, there is no ill intent within Him, His redemptive plan was initiated by His unconditional love and the power of redemption will be experienced by us based on our unconditional trust.

#394 *"Thanksgiving goes beyond the temporal and focuses on the eternal."*

If joy defies difficult circumstances and coexists with pain, then thanksgiving is a byproduct of joy. Thanksgiving extends our faith beyond our current need, knowing that God causes all things to work for the good to those who love Him and are called according to His purpose. Giving thanks is the purest form of worship because circumstances will not hinder or enhance its process, only a simple faith in God's good intentions in both blessings and trials. When thanksgiving takes place all hell breaks loose and holy ground is established in our hearts and beneath our feet; it is a gift from God that takes us from the now to eternity. We will be challenged with two conformities in life. We will either conform to this world or to the death of Christ. If we choose to conform to this world holiness is not our lifestyle and thanksgiving is not our spiritual service of worship. Circumstantial evidence will justify self-righteousness and Jesus will be a religious symbol in our minds but not Lord of our hearts. But conforming to the death of Christ in order to attain the resurrection from the dead reminds us daily that we have only just begun to know Him and the power of His resurrection and the fellowship of His sufferings.

This intentional lifestyle confirms what the will of God is, that which is good and acceptable and perfect.

TAKING ON SAINTHOOD

Chapter Twelve

Living Prophetic

Taking on sainthood involves living a prophetic lifestyle, where the word of God becomes our reality and truth is not just likable but livable. We may not all have the gift of prophecy, but we do have the power to live prophetically. So what does that mean exactly? It means God's word becomes our vocabulary and His purpose our plan. At any given moment Spiritual truth can be spoken to expose lies and deception brought to us by the enemies of our soul.

#904 "Too often we spend more time identifying our sin and how to avoid it, instead of proclaiming our freedom and how to enjoy it."

The prophetic word of scripture speaks volumes of how we have been liberated from our sin and empowered by God's love and forgiveness to overcome sinning again. Knowing that God cannot lie and that the devil is the father of lies is not just an encouraging word but the basis on which we believe. Had it not been for the Bible we would not know this to be true. Titus 1:1-3 says, "Paul, a bond servant of God and an apostle of Jesus Christ, for the faith of those chosen of God and the knowledge of the truth which is according to godliness, in the hope of eternal life, which God, who cannot lie, promised long ages ago, but at the proper time manifested, even His word, in the proclamation with which I was entrusted according to the commandment of God our Savior." In John 8:44 Jesus speaking to the Scribes and Pharisees says this, "You are of your father the devil, and you want to do the desires of your father. He was a murderer from the beginning, and does not stand in truth because there is no truth in him.

Whenever he speaks a lie, he speaks from his own nature, for he is a liar and the father of lies." All Scripture is inspired by God and profitable for teaching, for reproof, for correction, for training in righteousness; so that the man of God may be adequate, equipped for every good work. (2 Timothy 3:16-17) You cannot walk in the power of Christ without knowing the word of God. If we limit our scriptural vocabulary we will limit our power to overcome. In our flesh it does not take long to develop an ungodly vocabulary; if you spend time listening or reading words that are unwholesome you will find yourself thinking those words as you speak. Living prophetic is not just an option in constant Christianity it is a vital part of who we are in Christ. Jesus said if you abide in My word you are truly my disciples, you will know the truth and the truth will set you free. Disciples never stop learning and growing. When we speak the promises of God found in Scripture into our lives and the lives of others, we establish holy ground and God's love, mercy and grace is inserted in place of uncertainty and doubt. Self-control is intentional, when we choose to broaden our vocabulary with God's word we take spiritual control over our daily trials and temptations. This leads to teachable moments where our hope, that joyful anticipation of God working things out, is in play.

#39 *"Joy strengthens the spirit; worry paralyzes the soul, rendering you weak in facing life's problems."*

Jesus goes so far as to say in John 8:31 that if you do not abide in His word you are not His disciple, you will not know the truth and the truth will not set you free. I do not know about you but if God, through His divine power, has granted to me everything pertaining to life and godliness found in scripture, I am surely going to put on the armor of God and use the sword of the Spirit that is the word of God throughout my life. Once we commit to knowing the prophetic word of God our problems turn into object lessons that simply equip us with endurance and once endurance has its perfect result we will be complete lacking in nothing. Because our human nature is slow to grow and quick to regress in the midst of our transformation and the renewing of our minds, the prophetic lifestyle should be current with each new day. Your favorite scripture should be the last one that spoke change and challenge into your life.

#884 *"I don't know if you noticed or not but change is inevitable."*

Do not just *read* the Bible; seek out verses that will change and challenge you and the sphere of life around you. It is in those moments that the Bible studies you, giving you spiritual insight in a temporal world. We are called to be admonished and to admonish making spiritual sense out of temporal circumstances. Spiritual, physical and emotional change is inevitable, but in Christ, change for the better has been given to us who believe in each of these areas of life, the choice is ours. If you want to live in the Spirit you must also walk in the Spirit. What does it mean to walk in the Spirit? First of all walking takes initiative, balance and strength. If you are standing still you are living but not experiencing the fullness of God's power, you are not stepping out in faith to experience change and the challenges that compete with that change, trusting God through it all. Do not let people and circumstances initiate how you walk. To live prophetic is to walk in the Spirit and not carry out the desires of the flesh. If you wait to initiate your spiritual authority after trials or temptations take place you may have trouble catching up spiritually. But if you initiate spiritual authority throughout your day, standing on the word, praising God for nothing and conversing with Jesus for the sake of simply getting to know Him, when trials come your response in the Spirit will overrule reacting in the flesh. Instead of being challenged by the temporal you will be changed by the eternal, that is what making spiritual sense out of temporal circumstances is all about. Being changed by eternity takes a well-balanced walk with Jesus, being yoked with Him, walking in His steps. God does not call us to live high or low emotionally; emotions do not play a part in spiritual gain. Every day should be the same. "God is" and we fill in the blanks. This does not mean we live life emotionless, but instead we live self-controlled and joyful in the midst of trials. Care-less living would be a better description of living prophetically, not emotionless. Care-less living reflects liberty in the Spirit and is not feelings oriented.

#738 *"God always has a reason for the season, a plan for the pain and a way where there seems to be no way."*

Matthew 6:13 says, "And do not lead us into temptation, but deliver us from evil. For Yours is the kingdom and the power and the glory forever. Amen." When Jesus taught His disciples how to pray He gave them a pattern to follow. He concludes with, after it is all said and done, after you have measured the cost, realize that your choices can lead you into temptation. If I have made a mistake change my direction and deliver me from evil, for Your power is sufficient and Your glory is necessary for me to conquer my mistakes. David writes in Psalm 139:23-24, "Search me, O God, and know my heart; try me and know my anxious thoughts; and see if there be any hurtful way in me, and lead me in the everlasting way." The prophetic life knows the truth and trusts God's power in real time. The power of God is such a mysterious experience, He relies on us to depend on Him. Walking in the Spirit is a supernatural overflow of living prophetically. Knowing the truth of God's word precedes walking in the Spirit because it is the power source that initiates, balances and empowers us to become. Jesus at no time lacked power, but at times it took on different forms. He surrendered to the Father's will, way and timing, but He never relinquished it. Power is who God is and as His children it is who we are unto salvation.

TAKING ON SAINTHOOD

#1033 "Don't think beyond God's purpose and plan, don't speak until God has spoken and don't act outside of faith."

Taking on sainthood is a powerful expression of what happens when we build on our childlike faith. Paul prays this prayer in Ephesians 1:17-19 "that the God of our Lord Jesus Christ, the Father of glory, may give to you a spirit of wisdom and of revelation in the knowledge of Him. I pray that the eyes of your heart may be enlightened, so that you will know what is the hope of His calling, what are the riches of the glory of His inheritance in the saints, and what is the surpassing greatness of His power toward us who believe. These are in accordance with the working of the strength of His might." The spirit of wisdom and revelation are key to the prophetic lifestyle; knowledge is the accumulation of facts while wisdom is the application of knowledge. When the truth of God's word is applied to our life, change happens. The revelation of Jesus becomes our source of livelihood, God's word brings instruction and our faith establishes our eternal perspective. Pray daily for wisdom and revelation, which brings unending peace and joy in the Holy Spirit. In order for us to know the hope of our calling the eyes of our hearts must be enlightened, this is where the word of God instructs us how we should live. Not only remembering our inheritance in Christ but also the power that comes with God's call in Christ.

Verse 19 shares four different words for power demonstrating different ways God strengthens us throughout our day. The first word is **power** (dunamis in Greek). This is where we get the English word dynamite. Dunamis power is a physical display, the inherent power of God giving us the power to perform and achieve. It is a necessary strength that causes growth based on our acceptance of God's love, mercy, grace and forgiveness through the life, death and resurrection of Jesus. Dunamis has nothing to do with our ability to perform, but instead God's ability to perform through us.

If you find yourself without power in this world you are living in the wrong world.

#922 "*If you want to change your life change your perspective.*"

Jesus said, "Blessed are the poor in spirit for theirs is the kingdom of heaven." This is acknowledged poverty having little to do with wealth but instead position. We can be grounded in a world of hurt, or caught up in a heavenly kingdom where Jesus sits at the right hand of the Father and the surpassing greatness of His power enables us to become children of God.

The second word for power used in verse 19 is **working** (energeia in Greek) where we get the word energy. This power from God involves activity and influence in our lives. It is God's operative power, it is how prophetic lives operate; our activity reflects God's purpose, our influence demonstrates God's plan. At no time should we choose to be entertained by anything outside of God's activity and influence in our lives. That is what the word of God does, it keeps us spiritually involved in a temporal, physical, emotional world. When we choose to walk in the Spirit we choose to live in the kingdom of heaven making our time in this world holy ground.

The third word for power used in this verse is the word **strength** (kratos in Greek). It means the power that produces ability to complete or finish the task at hand. It also means to take dominion over. It is the power of being in control through the process God has set before us to finish His purpose and plan for our lives. Kratos generates and develops joy. Joy is not only the Fruit of the Spirit, a characteristic of God, but a fortress, a place of safety and refuge where we go and allow God's Spirit to minister to our spirit and make spiritual sense out of temporal circumstances. When kratos is functioning in our day to day we lead with joy and are trusting God's purpose and plan for the moment.

#351 *"Conflict can only cause pain when we choose to not trust Jesus but instead our ability to cope with the problem."*

The final word used for power is **might** (ischus in Greek). Power from God that overcomes immediate resistance from the enemies of our souls. Ischus is spiritual spontaneous combustion. It is the opposite of the emotions that react to circumstances based on feelings. In Christ we have the power to respond to God's pleasure without hesitation if we choose to do so. Ischus is important because it erases excuses, the skin of reason covering a lie, from our thought process. Not only are we responsible to live as children of God, we have the ability to respond in a spiritual and godly way at any given moment in time. Having the power to become is part of this response ability given to us by God. It is our rite of passage, delegated authority that overrules all challenges to our faith embodied in our freedom to choose. Living prophetically allows us to develop what we learn to be more than just students of the word, but also teachers. If we are not sharing with others the truth we receive from scripture we are no different than that Bible on the bedroom table accumulating dust, starving for acceptance.

#913 *"Opinions are of no value when God's wisdom is available."*

Sharing the prophetic word in scripture does not mean you know it all, only that God's wisdom has manifested itself to you for the purpose of spiritual clarity in an otherwise confusing atmosphere. It will always address the spiritual need in the moment. Once that is established, emotional and physical concerns can be sorted out with truth and not suggestion. God is still nourishing us daily as He did in the wilderness, a portion of wisdom every day enabling us to depend on His provision for the moment. The

Scripture says that the Holy Spirit teaches us all things and brings back to our attention that which was spoken to us. (John 14:26) Our relationship with the Holy Spirit takes time to build through the process of life. God followers become God leaders, God learners and God teachers. The Holy Spirit requires us to be nothing more than echoes of truth, He will do everything else through the process of living prophetically. God is responsible for how truth is received by others; our responsibility is simply to share what we learn. Rejection is never ours to receive when teaching others. The Holy Spirit is the source of all wisdom and when truth is rejected He lovingly looks for teachable moments to fulfill God's redemptive plan in us and the sphere of life around us.

#809 *"God keeps His word in the moment, we must live for that moment."*

When we take on sainthood prophetically and walk in the power of the Spirit, the liberty of life releases us to not be burdened with the unknown, but encouraged by the known will of God. Our rest is the enemy's unrest. The devil wants nothing less than to have us dwell on our interests and not the interests of God, to be distracted by the rejection of others and not the acceptance of Christ, to communicate our will instead of speaking the prophetic will of God. (Matthew 16:23) Remember: Life can be simple if we don't make it complicated.

Chapter Thirteen
Relevance

In a world filled with ungodly opinions and the lies of the devil developing it's morality, more than ever before the gospel of Jesus and the truth of God's word is necessary for us to learn and to teach the sphere of life around us. Jesus said you are either for Me or against Me, there is no middle ground when it comes to the gospel. Jesus is the separation between man's sin and God's holiness. Yet in this world middle ground is the standard by which they live. Where sin was once repented of it is now the normal, natural way of life. Love is love and God is irrelevant. The world seems to think it has out lived God's love, mercy and grace. There is no need for truth and if you question it's motives you have committed the sin of intolerance and your holiness is no more than bigotry. The lies of the enemy have produced the rotten fruit of the flesh in which there is no God, only a self-governing world overcome by the deeds of the flesh. If we as children of God do not stand for the truth of God's word we will offer up our children and grandchildren to the god of self, succumbing to the schemes of the devil. When we take on sainthood we must stay in the divine and focus on godliness. Holiness precedes power; it is not just a good idea or an alternate lifestyle that we can walk in and out of. Through Christ, holiness is what creates us to be and without it we are unable to become. Holiness is who God is and without it our adoption is invalid.

#513 "There's a difference between getting saved and living saved."

Living saved submits to the word of God, obeys the will of God and accepts the ways of God. Getting saved is void if living saved does not follow.

Submission, obedience and **acceptance** are three platforms in which we demonstrate the holy power of God. In Romans 8:7 the Bible tells us that the mind governed by the flesh is hostile towards God, it will not and cannot submit to God's law. In this world where relevance is a lie and it's government is the deeds of the flesh, to even consider God's holiness and truth found in Scripture is offensive to its bondage. The mind of man without Christ cannot and will not please God because to place faith in God is to repent from sin and change your heart and mind according to God's word. The world views God's word as foolishness, but to us who are being saved it is the power of God unto salvation. Submission is not a one-time experience in Christianity, it is part of living saved and staying in touch with God's purpose and plan for our lives. James 4:7 says, "Submit therefore to God. Resist the devil and he will flee from you." When we submit to God and the power of His word we receive the power of resistance against the devil. It is good to note the fact that the devil cannot force anyone to sin, he only gives us options to sin, the choice is always ours. But only in Christ do we have the power to resist the devil and he will flee, for demons shudder even at the sound of His name.

#384 *"Failing to be victorious in troubled times is caused by a lack of discernment, poor timing and wrong procedures."*

If we are not submitted to the word of God we will not be able to discern right from wrong; we will make choices based on feelings not facts, impatience will take the place of God's timing and circumstances will tempt us to react to what we see instead of what we know by faith. The relevance of truth is our reality, it should never be set aside to embrace sin in a lost world governed by compromise and hostile towards the cross of Calvary and all it represents. Obedience to God's word will also release the holy power of God in those who believe. I Thessalonians 5:16–18 says, "Rejoice always; pray without ceasing; in everything give thanks; for this is God's will for you in Christ Jesus." God's will for us is to always lead with joy, have an attitude of prayer and thank Him for everything. When these three things are part of who we are, we will demonstrate the holy power of who God is to a lost world wanting what we have but not obeying the God that died to provide it for them. Once again Jesus is our scriptural example of living saved in regard to obedience to the Father. His simple confession in the midst of redemption's plan was, "Not My will but Yours be done." He was tempted to change the time and process of redemption but knowing the word and heart of God He obeyed the plan set before Him, enduring the cross despising the shame. Obedience does not come without a cost. The life assurance that it provides cannot be found in this world, it's reward is in heaven. God will take us beyond this world and it's limited benefits that are irrelevant to eternity where Christ is seated at the right hand of the Father.

#397 *"Be deliberate and determined to love and worship Jesus daily."*

Accepting God's ways is a platform of faith that defies what we see in defense of what we know to be true in Christ. Isaiah 55:8-9, "For My thoughts are not your thoughts, nor are your ways My ways, declares the Lord. For as the heavens are higher than the earth, so are My ways higher than your ways and My thoughts than your thoughts." That being said, God is God and we are not. God does not have our emotional make up to battle with daily nor our sinful nature that questions our choices. Our understanding is based on our history and the cultural atmosphere in which we live. God has no history; He always was and always will be. He is the same yesterday today and forever. God has never had to change who He is, perfect love and holiness make up His character and there is no need for improvement. We must view God always with an assurance of things hoped for and a conviction of things not seen, trusting God and not leaning on our own understanding. Accepting God's ways in all things allows us to walk the straight and narrow without being intimidated by the broad road of inclusion. The reason we have such a hard time accepting God's will be done on earth as it is in heaven is because it takes faith that is out of this world and has nothing to do with our goodness and achievements. Our relevance has no valuable involvement in God's best for our lives, only our total commitment to trust, obey and accept God's plan, making everything we say and do in Christ relevant. It is vital for us to know that as we stay in Christ we stay relevant in the lost world shouting it's way over His way. Psalms 18:30-32 says, "As for God, His way is blameless; the word of the Lord is tried; He is a shield to all who take refuge in Him. For who is God, but the Lord? And who is a rock, except our God, the God who girds me with strength and makes my way blameless?" The devil would like nothing else but to convince us that we have nothing to offer the sphere of life around us, that we are inadequate and unworthy. Yet in Christ we are the righteousness of God, He made Him who knew no sin to be sin on our behalf. (2 Corinthians 5:21) To believe the lie of inadequacy is to reject the cross of Calvary. Do not think for a second that you, as a child of God taking on sainthood, are anything less than a King's kid. Our inheritance is strength and blamelessness, we will always be accused by the devil but his accusations should quickly be rebuked based on the word of God. So what is the key to our relevance? It is our unending pursuit of God's holiness, trusting His way over ours, believing that God is blameless and can do no wrong. His refuge is a safe place, not one where trials may not occur but where God and His unconditional love will never leave us or forsake us and meet our needs according to His riches in glory. The key to relevance is carefree living, where Jesus is the answer to all of our questions.

#859 *"Bad days happen when we reject God's way, when and how God wants it."*

To live carefree is to not put God in a box and limit His creativity working in and through us. Remember: Everything we go through in life is for the furthering of the gospel in us setting an example of faith for the lost world around us. Just as God's word is all about wholeness and witness our lives should reflect God's word based on our wholeness and witness. If we can get outside of ourselves and see the big picture of redemption, we will be better prepared to establish hope based on hope. Our feelings of inadequacy are based on our lack of preparation where faith is established. If God has your heart the devil cannot get your ear. So know this, God is relevant, making you relevant. In this world you will deal with tribulation but fear not for Jesus has overcome the world. God's love will cover a multitude of sins, cast out fear and never fail. Your sainthood is based on God's love; your thoughts, words and behavior must be based on God's love, anything less leaves you vulnerable to the schemes of the devil.

#13 *"A gentle spirit does not allow negative emotions to overrule spiritual responsibilities."*

In the book of Philippians chapter 4, Paul gives us the formula for relevance before God and man. Rejoice always, let your gentle spirit be known to all men, the Lord is near and be anxious for nothing. Paul goes on to say that through prayer God's peace will guard our hearts and minds in Christ Jesus. Lead with joy, a rejoicing heart reinforces God's presence and a gentle spirit reevaluates circumstances developing a calm perspective producing an awareness of God's power. Choosing not to be anxious or worry in all things becomes a position of strength and not weakness. Trials are inevitable, misery is optional. We view being anxious for nothing as a last resort instead of the third step in living a victorious life. Being anxious for nothing is proactive, it is not crawling out of the pit of despair but through joy, gentleness and peace stepping over the pit and not succumbing to the spirit of fear. There is not a single Bible verse that encourages a Christian to worry, only to know that God is in control even when things seem out of control. This is where patience comes in; it is the continuance power of the Holy Spirit and without it we will not trust the Father or His timing, making Hebrews 11:1, "Now faith is the assurance of things hoped for, the conviction of things not seen" a memory verse and not a lifestyle.

#30 *"Patience is accepting a difficult situation from God without giving Him a deadline to remove it."*

We tend to separate the temporal from the eternal but God holds both in his hand. When we keep our eyes on Jesus, faith is released and eternity is seen throughout our temporal circumstances. God can only want His best for our lives, there is no middle ground. Patience is an inward strength to withstand stress in accomplishing God's purpose in us. When we walk in the Spirit and partner with God's plan, relevance becomes a lifestyle and God's glory our objective.

Chapter Fourteen

In Jesus Name

There is a correlation between the name of Jesus and the power of God. Jesus represents authority, purpose and power from God. His name is not a religious formula that gives us what we want but instead a reminder of our need to surrender to God's will be done. Praying in Jesus name is not a catchall to get what we ask for but a position of authority accepting from God all that we need and embracing His presence so as to receive those needs. Having faith in God's holy purpose in prayer sets us apart from the world, leaving no hindrances for us to deal with. God, at our request, will provide based on His perfection not our perspective. The name of Jesus welcomes the prayer and releases God's power. When we focus on the problem in prayer we are viewing what seems to be as more significant than the healing that comes from the Father. It is not easy to separate the two but necessary when it comes to faith; the name of Jesus brings us the peace we need to allow faith in God to be perfected. The prayer of faith causes us to deal with the subject at hand not our vain imagination prompting us by feelings. Jesus felt sorrow and compassion towards those that He healed and so can we. Pity isn't compassion or sorrow but instead an emotional view of a person's condition. Pity may seem alright but it usually leads to negative feelings focusing on the problem not godly solutions.

#79 *"Faith embraces the providence of God."*

Faith professes what God promises, not just the promises that meet our needs or wants but also the promises that mysteriously touch our hearts even when nothing changes in regard to our needs. God's protection releases His provision spiritually; this is where He is most concerned. When we pray in Jesus name we acknowledge God's sovereignty, knowing that He hears us and will give us what is necessary based on His unconditional love, mercy and grace.

John 14:6 says, "...no one comes to the Father but through Me." Everything flows through Jesus name, the power that opened heaven on earth for us to receive the love of the Father. In John 14:14 Jesus says, "If you ask Me anything in My name, I will do it." And again in John 15:16 "You did not choose Me but I chose you, and appointed you that you would bear fruit, and that your fruit will remain, so that whatever you ask of the Father in My name He may give to you." We can do one of two things, demand that God obeys His word or trust in the power of Jesus to fulfill His way, truth and life in us as we share our wants and trust God to meet our needs. We must offer up our prayers with open hands not clenched fists. If we ask according to God's will, we will never be disappointed with God's answers. You may say that is not fair; no that is a relationship in which God is sovereign.

#463 *"God's reality does not depend on anyone for validation."*

If God is not in control we are out of control. Remember: Spiritual growth is God's priority. If there are no trials in our lives and no reason to be faithful, we will not be complete, lacking in nothing. Trials give us opportunities to rejoice and trust God's will in the midst of our wants so that we may be fruitful in our day to day. When we bear the fruit of the Spirit in our lives, our prayers will have as much to do with what it takes spiritually to get through the temporal trials we desire God to remove. When we pray in Jesus name we take authority against the flesh, world and devil and submit to the authority of God's best for us in whatever season of life we may find ourselves in, as well as the needs of those in the sphere of life around us.

#129 "Live each day with a working faith, laboring love and enduring hope."

God's truth is our reality, Jesus is reality in its purest form and if He is our spiritual life, we will spend less time adding up unanswered prayers and more time confronting our disobedience and disbelief, making every effort to glorify Jesus in what we think, say and do. Peter tells us in Acts 4:12 "And there is salvation in no one else; for there is no other name under heaven that has been given among men by which we must be saved." All trials leading to prayer are based on the resurrection of Jesus. We will succeed or fail in our trials based on two simple truths…Is Jesus alive? And is He alive in us? Our healing comes from God through the person of Jesus Christ. God's unconditional love releases our unconditional trust in Jesus name. Peter shares Acts 4:12 as a conclusion to circumstances found in Acts 3 where a crippled beggar asks for alms and Peter says in short, I have no money but I will give you what I have, in the name of Jesus rise up and walk. The beggar's ankles were strengthened and with a leap he began to walk and entered the temple praising God. This miracle gave Peter and John a platform to share that the power and piety of Jesus healed this man. Peter continues by teaching them the history of redemption starting with the prophets leading to the person of Jesus Christ, God's only Son. In chapter 4, Peter and John are confronted by the religious leaders and thrown into jail for teaching and proclaiming the resurrection of Jesus from the dead. But the Scribes and Sadducees were too late, 5000 heard their teaching and believed. The next day Peter and John were put before the high priest and asked by what power or in what name have you done this? Their response was Jesus whom you crucified, whom God raised from the dead, did this. And finally Acts 4:12 is spoken.

#149 *"Practice God's presence through prayer."*

Our confession will affirm God's presence and involvement in our lives or fuel the enemies attack against us. Praying in Jesus name is a simple reminder that Jesus is alive and active, able and willing to guide us with His Holy Spirit through the now and forever. The more we speak the name of Jesus the less we will be challenged by the demonic forces trying to deceive us with doubt and fear. James 2:19 tells us, "You believe that God is one. You do well; the demons also believe, and shudder." Add Jesus to your vocabulary throughout your day, do not wait for a reason to speak His name, just do it because that is faith at work. We can say thank you Jesus in any moment because He has done so much for us. So it is with praise you Jesus, He is worthy to be praised at all times, we do not need a pleasant experience or a church service to do that. Speaking the name of Jesus also reminds us of the abundance we have in the resurrected life He has given us. It is hard to grumble when you are thanking Jesus and praising His holy name. Finally Colossians 3:17 says, "Whatever you do in word or deed, do all in the name of the Lord Jesus, giving thanks through Him to God the Father." It is undone if it is not done in Jesus name. Do not take what you have for granted, always pray in the powerful name of Jesus and you will find rest for your soul and victory in your spirit. Once again we find scripture teaching us the importance of constant and complete identification with Jesus. We are to be anxious for nothing, no not one thing, we are to rejoice in everything, and whatever we do in word or deed, do all in the name of Jesus, giving thanks through Him to God! There truly is no middle ground in the kingdom of God. It is not safe to live on the borders of the kingdom, stay in the center of God's will and you will avoid borderline temptations.

#188 "Jesus never let people hinder His purpose, storms hinder His progress, and temporal circumstances hinder His perspective."

The whatever you do in word or deed in verse 17 leaves out nothing, all words and actions are done on purpose with Jesus in mind and heart. If we take a soul driven approach to life, emotions will rule and thanksgiving will be replaced with frustration, we will lose our eternal perspective, get caught up in borderline conflicts and relinquish the power of Jesus name, limiting our victory to self, which only leads to defeat for there is no power in our name. Hebrews 12:1- 3 tells us to "…run with endurance the race that is set before us, fixing our eyes on Jesus, the author and perfecter of faith, who for the joy set before Him endured the cross, despising the shame, and has sat down at the right hand of the throne of God. For considering Him who has endured such hostility by sinners against Himself, so that you will not grow weary and lose heart." Verse 7, "It is for discipline that you endure…" Verse 11, "All discipline for a moment seems not to be joyful, but sorrowful; yet to those who have been trained by it, afterwards it yields the peaceful fruit of righteousness."

We have a negative view of discipline based on our worldview. In God's eyes discipline has more to do with producing the peaceful fruit of righteousness and less to do with standing in a corner having a time out based on bad behavior. Discipline has to do with our pre-determination to live holy and to do whatever it takes to stay in the center of God's will. Discipline prevents timeouts based on bad behavior and glorifies God in all that we say and do in Jesus name, giving thanks through Him to the Father.

The name of Jesus empowers us to attain all godliness in regard to life's challenges. A disciple is a learner, one who through discipline makes godly choices in the powerful name of Jesus and teaches others the value of discipleship. It is for discipline that we endure. Endurance is produced through a lifestyle of loving Jesus and trusting in the Father's plan for our lives, no matter what it may entail. God's purpose and our progress and perspective are based on our willingness to lead with joy, embracing the name of Jesus in whatever it takes to become all that God has called us to be. We may deal with the sorrow of discipline, difficult times happen, but there is victory in the name of Jesus if we choose joy in the midst of trying times.

#6 *"Human happiness is often dependent on the chances of life over which we so often have no control."*

Life's twists and turns can catch us by surprise but should never catch us off guard. We should be prepared to rejoice at any given moment no matter what the surprise may be. It is all God if we keep our eyes on Jesus and not rely on happenings to secure our joy. Taking on sainthood is growing in respect to salvation. We are not saved by our works but we should not be ignorant to the fact that faith without works is useless. Faith is believing in Jesus and applying the principles of scripture that builds on that belief making spiritual sense out of our day to day trials, tests, and temptations, turning them into testimonies of God's faithfulness in Christ. 1 Peter 2:3-5 says, "..if you have tasted the kindness of the Lord. And coming to Him as a living stone which has been rejected by men, but is choice and precious in the sight of God, you also, as living stones, are being built up as a spiritual house for a holy priesthood, to offer up spiritual sacrifices acceptable to God through Jesus Christ." First of all there is no acceptable sacrifice to God outside of Jesus Christ, He is truly the only way to the Father. Jesus is the living stone, the foundation, the corner stone of redemption that this world rejected but the Father ordained as chosen and precious. In Christ we too now become living stones, a holy priesthood chosen by God to proclaim the excellencies of Him who has called us out of darkness into his glorious light, to offer up spiritual sacrifices acceptable to God through Jesus Christ.

What are the spiritual sacrifices that we offer in holiness? It starts with the Holy Spirit school of Christ that involves the invisible realm of God and embraces the fruit of the spirit, the armor of God, the word of truth, the leading of the heart and not the flesh. Spiritual sacrifices start in prayer and praise and are evident in word and deed. It has nothing to do with the physical world around us but instead God's Holy Spirit within us. Our faith in Christ allows us to worship for nothing, praying when there is no need and offering up spiritual sacrifices that glorify God because He is worthy of all our praise. Our lifestyle in Jesus name is our sacrifice, living each day come what may, equally yoked with Jesus, not distracted by what we see or what seems to be.

#8 *"When we speak of surrender, sacrifice and submission to God's will, we must keep before us the fact that Christ's purpose in our lives is to bring to us heavenly happiness starting here on earth."*

For those of us who have tasted of the kindness of the Lord, it is our responsibility to example the same spiritual discipline Jesus possessed while on earth. His spiritual sacrifice provided us with redemption, holiness before God in heaven while He fulfilled His purpose on earth. Our spiritual sacrifice will teach the sphere of life around us what it means to be in Christ on earth as it is in heaven. II Corinthians 5:21 tells us, "He made Him who knew no sin to be sin on our behalf, so that we might become the righteousness of God in Him." God truly has a first name and that name is Jesus. If the name of Jesus is not our first response to God we have missed the point of redemption. We cannot approach the righteousness of God outside of Jesus, and in Him we have been given the power to become. Purity precedes power and there is no other name given to men by which this power can be received.

TAKING ON SAINTHOOD

Chapter Fifteen

God Pleaser

Our human tendencies are to be liked and we usually live out our lives accomplishing those tendencies. That is why peer pressure plays such an important part in our growing up years and, if not curbed, will eventually seep into our adulthood. Too often bad choices are made when acceptance by peers is in the balance, someone caring about you is worth the crime in spite of the consequences. Unfortunately this mindset plays into the flesh of man, the ways of the world and the devil's schemes against us. When we live with such a limited perspective godly wisdom rarely plays a role in the decision-making process. Only our soul is satisfied and we become man pleasers and self-seekers . The slippery slope of wanting to be liked and accepted at any cost develops a self-satisfied lifestyle where emotions rule and feeling good is our ultimate goal. Remember: The choices we make, make us.

#227 *"Don't allow what you see affect what you know."*

Joy was the proclamation when Jesus came into the world. Everything changed when Jesus brought us the freedom to choose joy over all of life's challenges this world has to offer. "Joy to the world the Lord has come let earth receive her King." Luke 2:10–11 tells us "But the angel said to them, do not be afraid; for behold, I bring you good news of great joy which will be for all people; for today in the city of David there has been born for you a Savior, who is Christ the Lord." And in verse 14, "Glory to God in the highest, and on earth peace among men with whom He is pleased." When God sent His Son He gave us an option to choose; in Christ we can become God pleasers or remain man pleasers, we can embrace peace, the presence of God on earth or remain controlled by the spirit of fear limiting our perspective based on our happenings and not the joy of the Lord which is our strength. Unfortunately the tendencies to please others instead of God and feeling the need to be liked and accepted is a continual challenge for those who believe. Taking on sainthood needs to address these natural barriers and somehow enter into a supernatural life in Christ. This is where leading with joy comes into play. Joy has nothing to do with this world, it is a spiritual fruit only produced by God. It cannot be duplicated or manufactured, peer pressure cannot develop it, self-satisfaction will not produce it, being accepted and liked cannot create it. True joy can only be experienced by faith in Christ and disciplining the soul to respond to God and not be limited by the natural barriers of life.

A God pleaser is always swimming upstream in regard to human nature. The contrary currents of this world will tempt you to go with the flow, do not make waves and that worldly unity should always overrule truth and holiness. God pleasers stand alone yet never experience loneliness for where the Spirit of the Lord is there is liberty.

#949 *"Our life on earth is purely about us and Jesus, not us and us."*

We serve others by serving Jesus, the overflow of our relationship with Jesus is service to the sphere of life around us. Keeping Jesus first in our priorities will not only benefit others but keep us from falling into the pit of serving Jesus by serving others. A man pleaser excuses self-satisfying behavior for the sake of going with the flow in the name of Jesus. There is no godly ministry when worldly priorities are sought after and achieved. The spirit of fear is the rudder that leads such behavior and it is the spirit of fear that creates temporal sight as being more important than eternal perspective. Being quick to listen is replaced with being quick to react. Staying connected with God's love, power and a disciplined mind exposes and rebukes fear. Proverbs 29:25 says, "The fear of man brings a snare but he who trusts in the Lord will be exalted." God pleasers are exalted above and beyond temporal circumstances and are not afraid of the challenges set before them. The fear of man replaces God's love, and words and deeds reflect recovery not resurrection. It is in these moments that having friends and feelings are more important than faith in Jesus and walking in the Spirit. Vain imagination controls our reason and life centers on self and not Savior. Unfortunately in the world there are many pitfalls and snares. The key to living in the Spirit and pleasing God is our faith, trusting Jesus as we walk through the obstacle course called life. It is important to remember that faith should initiate a response to God and in doing so develop and strengthen us even more. The same pitfalls and snares in this world can be used to bring about joy and a more meaningful walk in faith. The writer of Hebrews tells us that without faith it is impossible to please God for we must believe that He is and a rewarder of those who seek Him. Two questions: Is Jesus Christ your all in all, or do you have a substitute teacher that misinforms you and tries to show you another way and a half-truth to get you by? And two, do you believe that God wants to reward you and that He is not hindered by your flaws but instead pleased with your faith? You see becoming all that God has called you to be is not an instant change but a gradual progression heavenward with our hearts and minds focused on and developed by Jesus Christ.

#800 *"You don't develop grace you embrace it, and in doing so develop character."*

Galatians 1:10 says, "For am I now seeking the favor of men, or of God? Or am I striving to please men? If I were still trying to please men, I would not be a bond-servant of Christ." You cannot serve two masters, if you are the servants of God your service will be to God and your relationship with the sphere of life around you will be centered on wanting God's best on their behalf.

God's word urges us to present our bodies as a living and holy sacrifice acceptable to God, which is our spiritual service of worship.

#498 "Look to Christ not the crisis."

It is not enough for us to be accepted by God through Jesus Christ but as new creations in Christ, present ourselves acceptable, living holy before God. Once hope enters our lives it becomes our responsibility to joyfully anticipate God's love, mercy and grace working in and through us. God takes everything personal, everything we think, say and do as unto Him. So in a sense we should take everything God says and does personally. Stop trying to analyze and understand everything that is going on in life and just stand fast in the liberty wherefore Christ has set you free and simply trust in the Lord with all your heart. Remember: Hope is our responsibility.

#996 "If God doesn't have all of our heart, soon He will have none of it."

Spiritual growth must be continual, Jesus said if you continue or abide in my word you are truly my disciples, (learners) you will know the truth and the truth will set you free. (John 8:32) God's ways are contrary to the world. Spiritual goals will not just evolve on earth; it takes determination on our part to become children of God. We have all the power necessary to be God pleasers, all we have to do is make choices for Christlikeness to happen. That is why constant Christianity is such an important part of taking on sainthood. When we choose to live life based on the constant of God's word, praise and prayer, we give little time to those things that are contrary to who we know God is. Not that circumstances will not provide challenges in life but when our hearts and minds are spiritually alert, we will choose pleasing the Father over satisfying self.

#336 "Live your life based on what God has created you to be not who you are in the process of becoming."

Knowing God's will and obeying God's word helps us to accomplish God's purpose, thus fulfilling our destiny.

King David writes to us in Psalms 13, "How long, O Lord? Will You forget me forever? How long will You hide Your face from me? How long shall I take counsel in my soul, having sorrow in my heart all the day? How long will my enemy be exalted over me? Consider and answer me O Lord my God, enlighten my eyes, or I will sleep the sleep of death, and my enemy will say, 'I have overcome him', and my adversaries will rejoice when I am shaken. But I have trusted in Your lovingkindness; my heart shall rejoice in Your salvation. I will sing to the Lord, because He has dealt bountifully with me."

David starts by questioning God's timing, concerned about whether or not He cares and looking for some visual response from God. Whenever you start feeling these emotions you are trending to a soul driven life and not a Spirit filled one. He continues by complaining about his enemies gloating over his misfortunes and his depression before he finally starts speaking spiritually into his circumstances. I trust Your kindness of love and rejoice in Your salvation; I will sing to the Lord because He provides for me bountifully.

#437 "When grace is acknowledged foolishness will stop."

The Bible tells us God's grace is sufficient, for in our weakness His strength will be perfected. (II Corinthians 12:9) It truly is foolish to give up on God, especially when He never gives up on us. He is perfect love and wants nothing but His best for us. Our Father will never do anything to harm, only to heal and to provide a safe and secure place for us to rest. Sin and it's residue causes much pain in the world we live in and if we could only choose God's spiritual plan for our lives, not based on what we see or feel but on what we believe to be true based on the love and sacrifice of Jesus, we could change the attitude and perspective of the sphere of life around us. It is commendable to come to your senses after giving in to a soul driven rant and praise God for His lovingkindness, but God has called us to do much more. That much more is found in the word of God. We have learned that God's word admonishes us, making spiritual sense out of temporal circumstances. Taking on sainthood makes spiritual sense before needing to come to our senses in regard to being a God pleaser. Let's change how we view the word of God; it is a preemptive attack against the enemies of our soul. Instead of us looking to scripture for answers in the midst of trials or temptation, let's already know scripture to use praising and thanking our loving Father in the name of Jesus Christ as a lifestyle in spite of trials and temptations. That is becoming; that is maturing; that is making spiritual sense out of temporal circumstances; that is rejoicing always and in everything giving thanks; that is the peace that surpasses understanding; that is the joy of the Lord that is our strength; that is love that casts out fear and covers a multitude of sins and never fails; that is the way, the truth and the life for those of us who believe. If Jesus said His truth will set us free, why are we entangling ourselves with the yoke of bondage? We need to discipline ourselves to walk in the Spirit. A disciple follows through with a commitment long after the emotions of making that commitment has passed. Pleasing God is a spiritual commitment to follow His lead no matter where the path may take us, staying true to His Spirit and not the emotional whims of our soul.

#310 *"We have a tendency to feel right past God when we don't trust His timing."*

We can hope for the best or be the best, the choice is ours.

Chapter Sixteen
Thy Kingdom Come

When Jesus came into this world He brought with Him a new morality: truth that was beyond anything we could possibly comprehend. No longer was darkness the only light found on the earth; Jesus brought with Him the light of holiness that opened the eyes of those who were blinded by this darkness. And it is only in this light that we find fellowship with God. John 1:4-5 says, "In Him was life, and the life was the Light of men. The Light shines in the darkness, and the darkness did not comprehend it." The darkness of this world is a lifestyle, a belief system that only entertains those things that help achieve temporal satisfaction, it knows no other way. But Jesus came with a new way, truth and life, and this life produced a holiness that brought us face to face with God. He took the now of temporal satisfaction and established the forever of eternal life. His kingdom is not of this world, darkness has no part of the kingdom of God, only the light of Jesus directing our paths to eternity. It is important to understand that darkness not only did not, but could not, take hold of the kingdom of God, the light and life of Jesus. For darkness to embrace light and make it its own would be to lose its power. Darkness will vanish if the light of Jesus is accepted. That is why John tells us He came to His own and His own received Him not, but to as many as received Him, to them He gave the power to become children of God or in its truest form children of light.

#17 "Purity keeps us focused on God's plan and not distracted by the lessons we must learn and the trials we must endure."

In John 8:12 Jesus says "...I am the Light of the world; he who follows Me will not walk in the darkness, but will have the Light of life."

"Thy kingdom come" is out of this world and cannot be overpowered by this world. It's foundation is truth and God's love initiates its purpose and fulfills its power. When we are chosen to be part of God's kingdom we see life as God intended it to be. The truth of God's word becomes the source of our day to day choices. There are no shadows of doubt when we are in the light as He is the light, only a spiritual trust in knowing and in knowing, wanting to know more, echoing the sentiments of Paul at the end of his life in a Philippian jail, to know Him and the power of His resurrection. I know at times it is challenging to see beyond the temporal when trials come calling, but it is in those moments that the power of God's purpose is most ready to be revealed. We must keep reminding ourselves "Thy kingdom come, Thy will be done, on earth as it is in heaven." Our spiritual fortitude will help keep our eternal perspective intact throughout our day to day. The dialogue that Jesus had with Pontius Pilate is very telling and we can learn much from this conversation. Pilate asked Jesus if He is the king of the Jews. In John 18:34, "Jesus answered, 'Are you saying this on your own initiative or did others tell you about Me'?" Who initiates our response to Jesus? Is it what others say or what we believe? Do we truly want to know the truth of the kingdom or just react to hearsay? If it is not personal it will not be powerful. Jesus continues the conversation in verse 36, "...'My kingdom is not of this world. If My kingdom were of this world, then My servants would be fighting so that I would not be handed over to the Jews; but as it is, My kingdom is not of this realm'." And verse 37, "...'You say correctly that I am a king.

For this I have been born, and for this I have come into the world, to testify to the truth. Everyone who is of the truth hears my voice'."

#415 *"Everything we say and do in this world should be motivated by our knowledge of heaven and what it takes to get there."*

Pilate thinks he is calling the shots, but Jesus already knows He will be handed over to the Jews. Too often we forget that God knows best and that our destiny is divine, it may seem like circumstances are calling the shots but we must not fear, Jesus came to overcome our world. It is the reason He was born and we are born again. Taking on sainthood is hearing the voice of God in Christ and obeying the truth of His word. When Jesus taught His disciples how to pray, Thy kingdom come Thy will be done was part of their daily communication with the Father after acknowledging His holiness. Think of what it would be like if every day started with, you are a holy Father, Your kingdom come Your will be done on earth as it is in heaven. Jesus is His kingdom come; Jesus was His will be done. Live each day as though it was your last on earth and heaven is waiting.

The kingdom of God is for us and nothing can stand against us, that is our reality, that is the truth. To everything there is a time and a purpose under heaven, a time to live and a time to die. This was Jesus' time to die, our redemption draws near. God's perfect sacrifice for the sins of man was about to take place, nothing on earth could stop God's will in heaven. The question must be asked, why would anyone reject God's love, mercy and grace? It is because those that are in darkness need to be in control no matter how much they stumble and fall. The story of Cain and Abel is a good example of darkness. Both present an offering to God; one is regarded and one is not. Cain becomes angry and the Lord goes to him and says in Genesis 4:6-7 "…Why are you angry? And why has your countenance fallen? If you do well, will not your countenance be lifted up? And if you do not do well, sin is crouching at the door; and its desire is for you, but you must master it." Cain rejects God's love, mercy and grace and kills his brother Abel. Abel on the other hand does the right thing and dies at the hand of his brother. Two men offer sacrifices to God, God blesses one and encourages the other not to lose heart. God loves them both but responds to each man differently. The darkness of Cain's soul rejects the light of truth and his anger leads to his brother's death. Able does nothing wrong and dies at the hand of his brother's sin. God's love will always provide a way where there seems to be no way. And our time on earth is limited to God's purpose in heaven, there lies our hope and faith in God's will be done on earth.

#492 "Love hopes for the best in the worst of times."

Hope releases a spiritual trust in God's control and knows where we stand in the end. If God is not in control then we are out of control! Jesus could have taken control in Gethsemane and allowed His feelings to form our destiny but instead, surrendered to the Father's love to continue through His sacrifice of redemption. He could have called down 72,000 angels to rescue Him from the mob, but chose to heal the ear of one of His captors. He could have shamed all those in court with His wisdom and their ignorance but chose to say nothing fulfilling God's purpose. Isaiah 53:7 says, "He was oppressed and He was afflicted, yet He did not open His mouth; like a lamb that is led to slaughter…" But Christ's death was not the end of God's redemption; in three days He rose from the dead validating His testimony of truth, releasing the power of God's love, mercy and grace to those of us who believe and have heard the truth and have been set free by it. If the resurrection validated God's redemption plan for man, wouldn't it be wise for us to live resurrected lives validating our relationship with Jesus and the fact that God's kingdom has come and we are experiencing the power of His love.

What initiates our thoughts, is it the resurrection or the limited understanding of what appears to be happening?

#908 *"Hearing is not enough, there must be applied learning."*

A disciple of Christ enters into a new way of life when Jesus is recognized, received and reverenced. God's kingdom in us overpowers the world around us. This just does not happen on its own, it comes through disciplined application of the truth of God's word. To hear is to forget, to apply is to learn. Listening to God's voice in the midst of hearing God's word conditions us to be more than conquerors and spiritually strong and devoted when trials come.

The kingdom of God within us overrules the world around us in regard to those things that are vying for our affection and attention. If Jesus is not on your throne you have heard but not applied the reason for truth. Taking on sainthood means giving an account of yourself to God in regard to how you have received and used truth to glorify the Father. Let's not forget that Calvary finished God's redemption on our behalf. When Jesus said, "It is finished," He was not referring to His life but to ours. The powers of hell and death were broken and everything pertaining to life and godliness became ours to receive and believe based on our experiential knowledge of Him who called us by His own glory and excellence (II Peter1:3)In order for us to be victorious in the present we must remember and believe God's past. We must remember that our Father's love gave us Jesus, the life of Jesus gives us power, the death of Jesus fulfills our payment for sin leading to holiness and the resurrection of Jesus sealed our inheritance as children of God. No longer do we conform in any way to the darkness of this world, but instead we are transformed mind, soul and spirit into the image of Him who called us out of darkness and into His glorious light. The Holy Spirit plays an important part in our redemption; Jesus said He will give us a helper when He ascends from this world. His helper will guide us in all truth and bring back to our attention that which was spoken to us. In other words, He will remind us of God's past in our present, giving us hope for our future. Everything we do in the moment has been prepared by God's past, all of our successes and failures come down to whether or not we believe God's kingdom has come and His will has been done on earth as it is in heaven.

#929 "When it comes to you, God can't do it without you."

Cooperating with the Holy Spirit enables us to be filled with the Holy Spirit. The plan of redemption was God's all along to be fulfilled, we had no part of that plan. Once redemption was accomplished we became a major part of God's purpose and plan. Our choices count. That is what freedom and liberty look like; partnering with Christ, submitting to God's word, being led by God's Spirit and glorifying the Father in word and deed. We become part of God's solution in our life, choosing the kingdom of God and submitting to His will be done. The Holy Spirit is a guarantee from God that provides wisdom and direction to those of us who believe. He is never wrong but relinquishes His rights to our will be done. When we submit to the Holy Spirit we can control our thoughts, control our whispers and in doing so control our disputes. The power we need to disciple our soul, mind and confession comes from the Spirit of God. Nothing can steal God's joy and peace from our hearts and minds, except our willingness to forfeit it to our circumstances.

#44 *"The thoughts we keep will help or hinder God's influence in our lives."*

Outside of the Holy Spirit there is no godly discipline in our lives. Knowing that our mind is the gatekeeper of our soul helps us to hold every thought captive if glorifying God is not its purpose. Jesus never allowed renegade thoughts to process in His life that would not help God's will on earth to be developed. Taking control of our thoughts reflects trust and surrender to the Holy Spirit's leading in our lives. When the Holy Spirit leads, joy is made full to whatever degree that joy is manifested. When Jesus stood before Pilate in silence, the joy of a calm delight penetrated the darkness of sin. This is the same joy found in Hebrews 12:1-2, "…Let us also lay aside every encumbrance and the sin which so easily entangles us, and let us run with endurance the race that is set before us, fixing our eyes on Jesus, the author and perfecter of faith, who for the joy set before Him endured the cross, despising the shame, and has sat down at the right hand of the throne of God."

Jesus created faith, He always saw beyond the temporal and lived in the eternal, He delighted in the calm of fulfilled purpose in the midst of the storms. It was His disciplined heart and mind that produced His endurance leading to our deliverance. God disciplines us for our good that we may share His holiness. If we do not embrace faith and the joy set before us we will never get to share God's holiness, only limited vision and temporal satisfaction leading to lost opportunities in taking on sainthood.

Chapter Seventeen

Perfect 10

When God gave us His rules for holiness to Moses on Mt. Sinai it was plain and simple. Moses was destined to fulfill God's purpose and plan for God's chosen people. He was far from perfect, but he was redeemed by God based on his call from God, and so are we.

Here are the rules for holiness beginning in Exodus 20:1-4: "Then God spoke all these words saying, 'I am the Lord your God, who brought you out of the land of Egypt, out of the house of slavery. You shall have no other gods before Me. You shall not make for yourself an idol..." verse 7, "You shall not take the name of the Lord your God in vain..." verse 8, "Remember the Sabbath day, to keep it holy." verse 12, "Honor your father and your mother..." verses 13-17, "You shall not murder. You shall not commit adultery. You shall not steal. You shall not bear false witness against your neighbor. You shall not covet your neighbor's house; you shall not covet your neighbors wife...or anything that belongs to your neighbor."

#909 *"The same standard that brought us to a knowledge of sin, will be used as a witness of our knowledge of Christ."*

When I view the 10 rules of holiness I am always amazed at their simplicity yet unattainable standard. It is only in Christ that we can embrace holiness, our sinful nature is too great for us to set aside on our own strength or merit. Jesus forgave our sins by fulfilling the law of holiness and once He succeeded, He gave up His life so that the law was no longer the judge of our eternity but rather Jesus, our resurrected Lord. Romans 3:19–20 tells us, "Now we know that whatever the Law says, it speaks to those who are under the Law, so that every mouth may be closed and all the world may become accountable to God; because by the works of the Law no flesh will be justified in His sight, for through the Law comes the knowledge of sin."

The 10 rules of holiness were given to us to reveal our sinful hearts and our inability to come to God and fellowship in His presence. They hold us accountable and speechless in our sin and ability to achieve holiness, the one thing that God requires for us to have fellowship with Him. But God's love gave us Jesus, the only one who withstood the test of time and achieved holiness in His life, fulfilling the law and providing for us a way to relate with the Father. It was in Jesus that the requirements of the law were accomplished and it is in Him that those same rules of holiness expose sin and now witness God's grace in us through Him.

#918 *"Grace is only significant when Jesus is served because of it."*

As we look at these plain and simple rules of holiness, let us not forget that our spiritual effort in accomplishing the perfect 10 is key to our witness, not so much our perfection in regard to the rules. If we make the effort God will make the difference through our trust in Jesus. If at any point in life we fail to pursue the 10, we have chosen to settle for the knowledge of sin and not the witness of God's grace in Christ through this holy standard of God. What good is it to know what sin is if we do not witness the grace of God that saves us from it? As we take on sainthood let's remember that our desire to *mature* involves the pursuit of *perfection*: these are interchangeable Greek words used in scripture. With God's provision of grace, excellence should be our top priority in achieving God's purpose and plan.

The 1st commandment tells us that God is God, "**You shall have and no other gods before Me.**" It is God who has delivered us from the bondage of slavery and has removed us from the sins of this world. Egypt represents everything that is contrary to God's purpose and plan. It is presented as a place where multiple gods are worshiped and freedom for God's people did not exist. Egypt was a place where the children of Israel were held captive, but they were first welcomed by Pharaoh because of Joseph and were prosperous in the land. A new Pharaoh who was threatened by their God and their success placed them in bondage. The change in government impacted the welfare of the Jews in Egypt, they no longer had the freedom they once possessed in the land and found themselves enslaved. America is a form of Egypt, once founded by scriptural truth, "In God we trust", but given to pagan rules we find ourselves, as Christians, being spiritually bound by ungodly standards and false gods. And just as the children of Israel fled Egypt physically we too have been led to freedom spiritually through our Lord Jesus Christ. The first commandment challenges us to live as God does; walking in the spirit of liberty, not being bound by the ways of the world but maintaining an eternal perspective. If Jesus is number one in our lives the first rule of holiness will not be hard to follow.

#910 *"Holiness and blamelessness comes to those who never stop continuing."*

Colossians 1:21-23 tells us, "And although you were formally alienated and hostile in mind, engaged in evil deeds, yet He has now reconciled you in His fleshly body through death, in order to present you before Him holy and blameless and beyond reproach-if indeed you continue in the faith firmly established and steadfast, and not moved away from the hope of the gospel that you have heard, which is proclaimed in all creation under heaven . . ."

Jesus said if you abide in My word you are truly My disciples, you will know the truth and the truth will set you free. (John 8:31) The word abide in the Greek text also means to continue. Our walk with Jesus and obeying God's word is continual; it should never stop or get put on hold for a season. Paul echoes that same thought to us in Colossians, if indeed you continue in the faith firmly established and steadfast, not moved from the hope of the gospel, you will be presented before the Father holy and blameless through Christ's life, death and resurrection.

The 2nd rule of holiness is **"You shall not make for yourself an idol."** An idol is anything that takes time and allegiance away from your personal walk with Jesus. We can make for ourselves a number of different idols in life. They have more of a spiritual significance than carvings of stone or wood. Hobbies, sports, work, family and church can all become idols when Jesus is not acknowledged as Lord in the midst of those activities. Our feelings can also take the place of faith resulting in emotional choices based on temporal circumstances and not on our eternal perspective. This soul driven behavior can easily become an idol in our day to day.

#905 *"Our pattern of life will determine our witness for Christ."*

What you get into gets into you, the habits you form will form you. Be careful how you think, speak and act; form godly patterns that ask the question, "Is my Father glorified?" Do not create places of worship where Jesus is not on the throne. The key to understanding the 2nd commandment is the term "make for yourself." When we become the creator of how we live in our day to day, false gods are formed and eventually worshiped. When man tried to take control of creation in Eden sin prevailed. Sin will always prevail when self creates our pleasure and not God. This rule of holiness can easily be used for God's glory by keeping our relationship with Jesus personal and making no provisions for the flesh to create. Somehow in life we must separate God's gift of creativity from the sin of idolatry, our idols in life may differ in many ways but all begin with and are centered on self. The 3rd command forming the perfect 10 is **"You shall not take the name of the Lord your God in vain."** Do not use the name of the Lord out of context, unseasonably and without reverence. The four-letter word for God found in the Torah was so holy that those who follow Jewish traditions do not pronounce it or even read it out loud but they instead proposed transcription forms such as "Yahweh" or "Jehovah". Terms such as Adonai (my Lord) or Hashem (the name) are used in addressing or referring to the God of Israel. YHWH, many modern scholars believe, comes from the Hebrew root words 'to be', 'to become' and 'come to pass.' When Moses asked Jehovah about His name in Exodus 3:14 Jehovah's answer was "I AM WHO I AM" or "I will be what I will be." Leviticus 24:10–16 tells us about an incident in which a man gets into an argument with another man and blasphemes the name and curses. He was then taken outside the camp and stoned to death. Verses 15-16 say, "You shall speak to the sons of Israel, saying, 'If anyone curses his God, then he will bear his sin.

Moreover, the one who blasphemes the name of the Lord shall surely be put to death…'." I have said all of that to say this: the holy God that created the universe and sent His only Son to pay the price for our sins has not lost His holiness in redemption. He is the same yesterday, today and forever. He will not and cannot change, except for His name. He is now a Father to the orphans and all those who speak the name of Jesus in reference to Him. He is no longer YHWH, four letters that brought fear and separation, but Abba (papa) four letters that proclaim love and acceptance in Christ. But let us not forget who our Father is in the rules of holiness that now in Christ allows us to establish a witness of His love, mercy and grace to the lost world we live in, always using the name of the Lord in context with His holiness, in season with His purpose and in reverence to His love.

#1049 *"If you lose your desperation, you weaken your development."*

As we take on sainthood do not take for granted our relationship with the Father and our holy walk with Jesus that has brought us to this moment in time. Never forget the despair that filled our souls before the Father bent a knee, sent His Son and delivered us from ourselves. Holiness and love go hand in hand, the words you speak in love will reflect purity and not vanity and when Jesus is lifted up He will draw all men to Himself. Let's be part of the solution and not the problem in a world that curses God by using His name in vain and not in worship. And when you pray, always pray in the name of Jesus; outside of His powerful name we have no audience with the Father. Too often I hear well intended prayers as though good intentions are worthy of any response from God if Jesus is not the center of our prayerful relationship. That, my friend, is vain imagination reflecting a lack of respect and ignorance in regard to the price Jesus paid and the need to never forget that holiness producing a right relationship with God is found in Jesus. When we pray in Jesus' name it is not a religious exercise but a reverent response to who we are in Christ, how we got here and the assurance that our Father will hear our prayers and meet our needs according to His riches in glory.

The 4th rule of holiness is **"Remember the Sabbath day, to keep it holy."** Throughout Scripture the seventh day was designated as a day of resting from all works. Its significance was found in the creation story in which God rested on the seventh day. When Jesus rose from the dead on Sunday a new day of rest was established in the Christian community. People started gathering and worshiping on Sunday, most businesses would shut down and people would take a day off from work on the first day of the week.

But the Sabbath rest has so much more to it than not going to work, it involves a holy rest spiritually that takes into account a lifestyle, not a 24-hour period of time.

#937 *"You will know God is at work in you when every day is a Sabbath rest."*

Hebrews 4:9-11 says, "So there remains a Sabbath rest for the people of God. For the one who has entered His rest has himself also rested from his works, as God did from His. Therefore let us be diligent to enter that rest, so that no one will fall, through following the same example of disobedience." Our Sabbath rest involves trusting God's accomplishments on our behalf: believing that Jesus is enough, redemption is true, the spirit world is real and the power to become and overcome is ours by faith. A Sabbath rest says nothing can separate us from the love of God. We should no longer struggle with the trials set before us and try to work through them with our own initiative, resolve or power. Our works should be a work in faith, a belief system that trains our soul to submit to God's will be done. The power of God will never leave us or forsake us no matter what our eyes tell us. Trusting Jesus through it all establishes a Sabbath rest and allows us to work out our salvation with reverence to God's holiness, knowing that it is God who is at work in us to will and to do according to His good pleasure. And His good pleasure will never disappoint us, for the love of God has been poured out into our hearts by the Holy Spirit that was given to us. The 5th rule of holiness tells us to "**Honor your father and your mother.**" This is where the rules of holiness take on a different form for it is no longer addressing our upward relationship with God, but instead, our relationship with those in the sphere of life around us based on our personal walk with Jesus. How we were treated as children can play an important role in how we witness the love and forgiveness of Jesus in response to honor on behalf of our parents. How we obey this commandment depends on doing what is right, not justifying wrong based on who is right. How we are or were treated by our parents has nothing to do with our responsibility to honor them.

#608 *"Are you living proof of what can take place in the life surrendered to Jesus?"*

The behavior of others should have no influence on our behavior towards them. When we do all things as unto the Lord, we do what is right remembering that while we were yet sinners Jesus loved us enough to die for our sins allowing the forgiveness of God to change our destiny; witness that change.

The 6th rule of holiness is "**You shall not murder**." This command seems obviously clear, do not murder anyone, but let's look at what would lead someone to take another's life, if not even their own. Several soul driven emotions come into play: anger, disappointment, jealousy, embarrassment and vengeance just to name a few. If these emotions are not held in check the power of forgiveness will be eroded leading to renegade thoughts, unwholesome words and eventually physical harm.

Jesus brings clarity to this commandment in Matthew 5:21-24, "You have heard that the ancients were told, 'YOU SHALL NOT COMMIT MURDER' and 'Whoever commits murder shall be liable to the court.' But I say to you that everyone who is angry with his brother shall be guilty before the court; and whoever says to his brother, 'You good-for-nothing,' shall be guilty before the supreme court; and whoever says, 'You fool,' shall be guilty enough to go into the fiery hell. Therefore if you are presenting your offering at the altar, and there remember that your brother has something against you, leave your offering there before the altar and go; first be reconciled to your brother, and then come and present your offering."

Jesus equates anger with murder in a spiritual sense and should be punished as such. Feelings of jealousy, embarrassment, frustration and disappointment feed into the anger of man and anger does not achieve the righteousness of God. (James 1:20) We must discipline our souls to reject such negative emotions from our thought patterns; unforgiveness will undo everything Jesus died to accomplish. Jesus even tells us when we are presenting an offering or in a place of worship (hopefully it is your lifestyle) if someone has something against you, make it right as much as it is possible for you to be at peace with all men. Romans 12:21 says, "Do not be overcome by evil, but overcome evil with good." As we take on sainthood a gentle forgiving spirit needs to be established in us so that when tempted with murder we will do the godly thing.

#611 *"Our words to each other should be in direct relationship with our praise to God."*

The 7th rule of holiness is **"You shall not commit adultery."** Adultery was a sexual, physical sin committed outside of the marriage seat. According to Leviticus 20:10 the penalty for adultery was death. Jesus takes this holy rule and raises the standard a few notches in Matthew 5:27-28, "You have heard that it was said, 'YOU SHALL NOT COMMIT ADULTERY'; but I say to you that everyone who looks at a woman with lust for her has already committed adultery with her in his heart." Lustful thoughts equate to adultery; you no longer have to commit the physical sin, just think about it. So as we take on sainthood, what is Jesus teaching us? That as a man thinks in his heart so he is, that thoughts do count, that we must hold every thought captive in obedience to Christ and that we must destroy vain imagination that does not give God the glory. Jesus raised the standard but He also did us a favor because thoughts lead to actions; it is better to repent from a lustful thought, if it gets that far, than it is to repent from the physical act of adultery. Genesis 3:6 shows us the first pattern of sin after the devil has the ear of Eve; once a thought is not held captive in obedience to her knowledge of God, she saw, delighted, desired and partook. There is another important aspect of adultery: God's children lusting after the world and its pleasures and riches. The spiritual sin of adultery against God is found throughout the Old Testament where high places were created to worship the pagan gods of the time. Even while Moses is receiving the perfect 10, God's people were making and worshiping a golden calf; it seems unthinkable but our human nature is drawn to the temporal and visual more than the spiritual. That is why we were given the Holy Spirit to admonish us as we go through our journey in this world. The choices we make will either strengthen our spiritual walk with Jesus or weaken our resolve when it comes to the sin of adultery.

#621 *"Holiness means submission to Christ, obedience to His word, surrender to His Spirit and service to all."*

The 8th rule of holiness is **"You shall not steal."** We all know what it means to steal something physically but it is the spiritual and emotional aspect of stealing that creates a void, enabling the soul and hindering the Spirit. The devil would like nothing better than to steal our joy, leaving us weak and unarmed. Not only joy, but it is the enemy's goal in life to steal the fruit of the Spirit. If he can get us to relinquish the characteristics of God by magnifying the temporal over the eternal, our witness will be shallow and soul driven instead of Spirit lead. The devil is always trying to deceive believers into being part of his scheme. Be an encouragement to the sphere of life around you, build up do not tear down the lives of those that Jesus died to save. Think and speak healing into their lives. To steal the joy of others is to deprive them of the power of God for them to become. That is why it is so important that no unwholesome word proceeds out of our mouths except that which produces edification, that it may bring grace to those who hear it. (Ephesians 4:29) Do not succumb to pity parties for this shows a lack of spiritual endurance and opens the door for the devil to give you sympathetic options that have nothing to do with God's will on earth.

#566 *"A true reflection of a trusting heart is a life of joy."*

Let us not forget that Jesus is our hope of glory and hope is that joyful anticipation of God at work in our lives.

The 9th rule of holiness tells us, **"You shall not bear false witness against your neighbor."** We lie for all the wrong reasons, the ongoing debate in life is if lying saves lives is lying ok? I understand the debate. When Nazi soldiers came to homes hiding Jews or when slave owners sent plantation foremen in search of runaway slaves at homes run by the underground railroad and those protecting them lied about their whereabouts, lives were saved. Domestic violence is another cause of alarm in which lives are saved based on lies. I do not have the answers as to how that works, all I know is that Jesus never lied and that lenience gives way to license. When is sin not a sin? When is it that we justify breaking God's holy rules based on our circumstances? I think the bigger more realistic picture is do we lie to our neighbor? Is our comfort zone more important than the truth? You see if we negate the value of truth based on the history of others, we will weaken the power of truth in His story and justify sin based on others circumstances. Taking on sainthood is waking up every day standing on the truth of God's word, being led by His Spirit and speaking the truth in love, growing in every aspect of Jesus Christ. This is how we obey the 9th commandment, not debating what was or what could be but being a witness of truth, trusting God for wisdom through each circumstance that arises in our lives and living for the moment.

The 10th rule of holiness is, **"You shall not covet your neighbor's house; you shall not covet your neighbor's wife...or anything that belongs to your neighbor."** Covetousness is contrary to contentment. Wanting what is not yours to have leads to renegade thoughts that release the devils power of persuasion. Be content with God's plan for your life. Viewing the sphere of life around you with holy eyes turns the 10th commandment into an opportunity to serve and not be served. Self becomes servant and what God used to reveal our knowledge of sin can now be a witness of God's love, mercy and grace. As with all the previous commandments, our faith plays into our perspective and lifestyle. We need to pre-determine what is right and do it prior to the temptation of lust and ungodly wants. If temporal satisfaction is your focus, contentment will be lost and you will fall prey to the lies of the devil. I Peter 5:8-9 says, "Be of sober spirit, be on the alert. Your adversary, the devil, prowls around like a roaring lion, seeking someone to devour. But resist him, firm in your faith, knowing that the same experiences of suffering are being accomplished by your brethren who are in the world."

#183 "Our faith places truth, righteousness and the gospel of peace as judge over our thoughts, circumstances, trials and temptations."

Chapter Eighteen

Living in the Now

The Bible tells us that this is the day that the Lord has made, we should rejoice and be glad in it. Jesus said today is the day of salvation (or healing). I am speaking on spiritual terms. I understand the value and necessity to prepare financially for our future, making choices that will provide for financial security is important. But this book is not about our financial investments or retirement but instead spiritual fulfillment. Living in the now has nothing to do with yesterday's successes or failures, nothing to do with tomorrow's blessings or trials, it is not what you did or will do in life but what you are currently doing. Living in the now is what makes constant Christianity so powerful: it lives in the present, eliminating the past, giving us hope for the future.

#169 *"What we see can deceive us, what we know will deliver us."*

II Corinthians 5:7 says, "For we walk by faith, not by sight." The lies of the enemy are 'seeing is believing' followed by 'where is your God now?' It is like this awesome loving all powerful God, who gave up Himself to save us from our sins and has given us the power to be, all of a sudden changes His mind and runs away from our circumstances. When you put it that way, you can see how absurd such a lie creating a thought in our minds can be. The idea that seeing is believing, when God's word says it is not, should be our first clue that we are being attacked. If we are not insulted by the lies of the devil, we are not living in the now and had better dust off our armor and put it on and while we are at it, put on the Lord Jesus Christ and make no provision for the flesh in regard to its lust. Remember: Believing is seeing. You begin living in the now when you pray before the need to pray, study before an occasion to apply God's word is necessary and worship before acknowledging God becomes an emergency. Just as God does not change based on circumstances neither should we. We cannot wait for circumstances to arise before we make that choice, but choose the holiness of Jesus prior to, not in the midst of trying times. That is what a personal relationship with Jesus is; talking to Him about nothing, worshiping Him because He is worthy, studying His word in a genuine, innocent, no strings attached desire to know Him. To be and not to do, that is the problem. We all want the blessings of God, but are we willing to bless God in the midst of our needs? That is what living in the now means: care-less, fulfilled, content and trusting. Peace does not involve presents from God but the presence of God. That is where the assurance of things hoped for the conviction of things not seen creates in us a faith that withstands every trial and temptation for His glory. God does not have to speak in order for us to listen, applying what we know delivers us from what seems to be.

#239 *"Patience reaches beyond the trials of the moment to see the fulfillment of the promise."*

Every generation from the beginning of man represents the now generation, that is our worldly inheritance; impatience. We have taken this inheritance into our Christian walk and instead of living in the now and believing that God causes all things to work for the good to those who love Him and are called according to His purpose, we want healing now, comfort now, deliverance in the natural now, setting aside the truth of God's word for temporal satisfaction. Do not let the trials of the moment distract you from God's fulfilled plan and purpose for your life as you rejoice in and through those trials.

There are three emotional challenges that hinder our spiritual progress in the now: **difficulty**, **delay** and **denial**. We are happy Christians when everything is going our way, but happiness is not our goal, joy is. A happy Christian is easily tripped up by **difficult** circumstances, but those same difficulties bring out the joy in those that are living in God's presence. Knowing that in those moments we get to prove God is. That is why we have been called and positioned in this world, to walk in liberty and to prove God's reality. If we do not embrace difficulty we are rebelling against maturity and purity. No one keeps a secret like God, and when Jesus comes into our lives He whispers in our ears, 'can you keep a secret?' Living in the now is keeping a secret, in the midst of difficult times. God will use those difficulties for the good. I do not know when and I do not know how, that is God's secret and I'm going to keep it, because I have faith in Jesus. God's word reveals to us the plan of salvation, the qualities of life that will strengthen us and determine our future, step-by-step instructions on how we are to live. But the process that God chooses for each of us to accomplish His purpose is not the same, it is God's secret. Have faith in God's secret plan for your life and you will live in the now, using difficulties as steppingstones leading to heaven. Which by the way is a secret place that we cannot even imagine. Psalms 91:1 tells us, "He who dwells in the secret place of the Most High shall abide under the shadow of the Almighty. I will say of the Lord , 'He is my refuge and my fortress; My God, in Him will I trust'." (NKJ) Let that be your emergency 911 call in the midst of difficult times; living in the now trusts in God's secret plan for our lives.

The second emotional challenge that hinders spiritual growth in the now is **delay**. This emotion feeds into the now generation before redemption. Delays in the now generation stirs up our soul to react to God's timing and eventually question God's purpose. Let's take a moment to acknowledge this important aspect of living in the now. God's sole purpose in our life is not to satisfy us but to sanctify us.

And His timing is a tool He uses to set us apart for His service. Living in the now understands that our time is not God's, a day is as 1000 and those who wait on the Lord renew their strength.

#198 *"Feelings are the most misleading excuses for not being responsible in our world."*

We have a tendency to feel right past God, when we do not have trust in His timing. And this lack of faith causes us to lose our composure. Reacting in the flesh and not responding in the spirit is a sure sign of someone who chooses happiness over joy, turning trials into burdens instead of an opportunity to develop maturity and purity.

The third emotional challenge that hinders living in the now is **denial**. Our best example of denial is Peter in the courtyard where he denies knowing Jesus three times before the rooster crows. We may say 'How can Peter deny Jesus in His greatest time of need?' It is simple, when we mistrust God's presence we deny His wisdom and power. God feels our pain, but is not damaged by rejection, only we are damaged by choosing to deny Jesus in the moment. Even Jesus, when He walked the earth, was amazed by man's lack of faith. He was not depressed by it because He came to give us the power to choose sin or Savior. Our lack of faith hurts us and the sphere of life around us, not God. When we choose to die to self and live for Jesus, we repent of denial and choose to glorify God, accepting His plan for our lives. No matter how mysterious life may become we never stop believing God's will be done on earth as it is in heaven. When we repent of denial we see things from a spiritual perspective and make choices based on God's wisdom and strength in the now and forever.

#324 *"Your joy in the present depends on your security of the future."*

Remember: You can be convicted but not convinced! Until you are convinced that Nehemiah 8:10, "…For the joy of the Lord is your strength" is for you, you will not truly live in the now. You may fake it on a bad day, believe it on a good day but never truly embrace God's unconditional love and give him unconditional trust in your daily walk come what may. I am convinced that living in the now understands the power of praise in good times and bad times, in sickness and in health and through it all believing we have been redeemed by the blood of the lamb. The power of praise sets us free from the barriers of this world and allows us to walk above and beyond the temporal. When you are confident of your future with Jesus, joy in the now is a supernatural response to God, knowing that nothing can separate us from His love and trust does not come through understanding but believing in His love, untouched by the downside of heaven. When Jesus prayed to the Father, "Not My will but Yours be done," He saw the joy set before Him, the fulfilled plan of our redemption, the resurrection and eventual ascension into heaven to sit at the Father's right hand. If we cannot see the joy set before us we will always be hindered by the temporal world we live in. Here is the difference between the now generation and those believers living in the now: one lives for today-eat, drink and be merry, the other lives for eternity. Jeremiah 29:11 says, "For I know the plans that I have for you 'declares the Lord', plans for welfare and not for calamity to give you a future and a hope." This promise was given to the children of Israel when 70 years of captivity had passed in Babylon. In the midst of their captivity by a pagan government God's plan had not changed. A hopeful future is always God's purpose in our lives. If you believe that, you have stepped into the now where Jesus walks.

#906 *"Our joy should always be determined by God, not our circumstances."*

God's delays are not always God's denials, and God's purpose will at times overrule our prayers. God is quite aware of our circumstantial needs, always seeing the big picture and knowing what is best for us in the long run. We may want to sprint to the finish line of resolution while God's desire for us is to go the extra mile, not only to develop in us endurance but to also touch the sphere of life around us on the pathway to maturity and purity. Prayer is such a mysterious part of our walk with Jesus. We pray and let our requests be made known to God, believing that He is and that He is a rewarder of those who seek Him while still holding true to His sovereignty. Father knows best and His purpose will always take precedence over our prayers. No matter how knowledgeable we are of God's word, we are still children in need of guidance when it comes to the big picture. I am convinced that how we respond to God in the midst of unanswered prayers is key to our endurance in the now. If you are walking in the spirit of liberty with Jesus, a no from the Father is not a bad answer, it is God's will be done; it is a *God* answer. And anytime God speaks we need to listen and rejoice; the extra mile is not a bad thing, it is what took Jesus to Calvary and beyond.

#222 *"The second mile will turn hassles into hopes and tests into testimonies."*

To everything there is a season and a time and a purpose under heaven. The Father never wastes time; living in the now embraces God's timing and with it comes hope and testimony. Do not let trials cause you to lose sight of God, but instead let them magnify His presence, that is what taking on sainthood does. If you are not rejoicing in what God is doing, then you do not understand what God has done. Every moment of every day brings us closer to the fulfillment of God's plan for our lives. To hesitate for a moment is to hinder praise and worship unto God. It is the plan of God in our lives that makes life worth living in the now. We are not here for any other reason but to worship our Lord and Savior and in doing so, glorify the Father in all things.

#334 "In God's perspective problems don't have sizes only solutions."

There can be nothing more exciting than to know God is with us at all times. All of our activities should be experienced with a simple whisper, "Thank you Jesus," that keeps life in its proper perspective: eternal. The same prayer that led to our redemption in Gethsemane should be our confession daily, not my will but Yours be done. Jesus was ruled by the Father's will and when given a choice He chose us. If we can get past our own temporal wants and surrender to God's eternal will, life will take on a new meaning. Living in the now should be filled with enjoying the journey, knowing God's will is what gets us to heaven.

Chapter Nineteen

Can You See Me Now?

Throughout the gospels when Jesus was spending quiet time with His Father He was making Himself visible to the world around Him. Visibility is necessary, the Bible tells us without vision the people perish. God's plan of redemption was to bring enlightenment to a darkened world lost in sin. Jesus is light and His children are bearers of light. If we want to impact the sphere of life around us we must see God for who He is in the midst of darkness. Without faith it is impossible to see God for we must believe that He is a rewarder of those who seek Him. Holiness is key to spiritual vision and faith heals the cataracts that cloud up our perspective. God is Spirit, and where the Spirit of the Lord is there is liberty. Spiritual vision is necessary for us to be set free from the barriers of circumstances. Seeing is not believing-it is just the opposite, believing is seeing.

#313 "Our lives in comfort or affliction should always produce comfort and not affliction."

The apostle Thomas is a good example of how seeing is not believing. He speaks only three times in the gospel of John and each time the significance of his love and loyalty to Jesus is highlighted. John 11 says that Jesus tells His disciples that He will be going to Judea because their friend Lazarus has died. The disciples remind Jesus, as though He needs reminding, that the Jews sought to stone Him to death. Jesus reassured them that this will benefit their faith. In John 11:16 the Scripture says, "Therefore Thomas, who was called Didymus, said to his fellow disciples, 'Let us also go, so that we may die with Him'." Thomas did not quite understand the fullness of

God's timing, but he did trust God's purpose. While the apostles struggled with God's plan, he believed and accepted following Jesus even if it led to death. His courage was encouraging and his confession had to have inspired the apostles because there is no argument or debate, only trust and obedience. At this moment in time, believing was seeing, leading to witnessing the miracle of Lazarus being raised from the dead.

The second time Thomas speaks in scripture is found in John 14; Jesus is telling His disciples that He must go, but He has prepared a place for them and He will come again and receive them to Himself. In verse 5, Thomas asks a question leading to one of the most profound statements found in Scripture. "Thomas said to Him, 'Lord we do not know where You are going, how will we know the way'?" In John 14:6, "Jesus said to him, 'I am the way, the truth and the life; no one comes to the Father but through Me'." God welcomes our questions when asked in innocence, profound answers will change the course of our day to day. The other disciples accepted ignorance, but Thomas pursued clarity and was given truth beyond his reality. Taking on sainthood is seeing Jesus in a personal way, truth and life. Jesus took a question of location and direction and made it personal between Himself and Thomas.

#62 *"Understand His truth, understand His sovereignty, then live life as though you do."*

Do not let what you see in life hinder your sight; just keep your eyes on Jesus and He will direct your path.

The third time Thomas speaks is after the resurrection when he is told that Jesus is alive. John 20:25 says, "...'We have seen the Lord!' But he said to them, 'Unless I see in His hands the imprints of the nails, and put my finger into the place of the nails, and put my hand into His side, I will not believe'." Thomas lost sight of Jesus; he could not see God's reality based on the circumstances. His response is one of discouragement and confusion. I am sure he wanted to believe, but he forgot how. His innocence was shaken, his faith limited to the trial set before him and disappointment ruled his soul. Eight days had passed and Jesus visited His disciples again. His greeting, 'Peace be with you,' was a reminder to them that His presence brings peace not the circumstances surrounding them. His first response is to Thomas, John 20:27–29 says, "...'reach here with your finger, and see My hands; and reach here your hand and put it into My side; and do not be unbelieving but believing.' Thomas answered and said to Him, 'My Lord and my God!' Jesus said to him, 'Because you have seen Me, have you believed? Blessed are they who do not see, and yet believed'." Seeing is not believing; believing is seeing. Jesus kept it personal and He did not do a teaching on doubt. Instead He simply healed Thomas by speaking the truth in love.

#83 *"Faith does not surrender to the flesh nor finds any reason to do so."*

Thomas let his emotions get the best of him and Jesus asked a simple question, 'Can you see Me now?' We all have those moments in time when our soul takes control. That is why it is so important for us to walk in the Spirit where believing is seeing and peace is not the absence of conflict but the presence of God. Do you realize that every good work we do based on God's goodness is created out of need? Help comes where help is needed. The opposite will always win over the opposition when we see God at work in our lives. Love casts out fear, peace overcomes anxiety, joy replaces sadness, hope overpowers discouragement and Jesus reigns in the center of it all. Jesus is not just a good idea, He is the only person that has experienced our challenges in life and yet without sin. He came as God, but He needed to live in our opposite world as a man so as to prove holiness can exist through faith and communion with God. He told His disciples if you have seen Me, you have seen My Father. To lose sight of Jesus is to lose perspective and our confidence in knowing that God is in control. Matthew 5:3 reminds us that blessed are the needy in spirit, for theirs is the kingdom of heaven. When we stop needing Jesus, we lose sight of His spiritual power and presence. We also neglect our spiritual power to become children of God. Remember: Becoming never stops and faith is necessary until we enter the kingdom of heaven.

When faith becomes sight and the unknown becomes our reality, we will see Jesus face-to-face. I Corinthians 13:12 says, "For now we see in a mirror dimly, but then face to face; now I know in part, but then I will know fully just as I also have been fully known." What is the "then" in this verse? I Corinthians 13:9–10 gives us a clear understanding, "For we know in part and we prophesy in part; but when the perfect comes, the partial will be done away." I know that we are not perfect, but living partial only hinders God's perfect outcome. If you cannot see Jesus in your day to day, it is not God's fault because He has given us all the tools necessary to view life from an eternal perspective and to overcome our temporal circumstances with godliness.

#252 *"Two things happen every time Jesus is revealed; we see truth more fully and the need for grace more assuredly."*

When Jesus rose from the dead, He fulfilled the truth of God's revelation and bestowed upon us the unmerited favor of God's redemption. The same grace and truth has now become our reality. It is our worship to God; there are many ways to get by but only one way to get real. Seeing Jesus in our day to day is not an option but a necessity. If we train our minds to think of Jesus when there is no emergency and to see Him in our day to day, we will be current when trials come and questions need to be asked of Him. We do not always have to live life on a need to know basis, let your faith know what is needed and you will see Jesus in the darkest storms. Then your questions will not involve doubt or fear but clarity and innocence. Our peace will be a person not a place and worship will not be hindered by our prayers.

#291 *"Who we are is determined by what we choose to believe."*

If faith is the conviction of things not seen, then who we are should be determined by our belief system, believing is seeing. Hope always sees the joy set before you producing endurance for the moment. Our response to God's intentions in every circumstance will either develop us His way or another. Who we are is an ongoing lesson in the school of Christ if we are not building our faith through spiritual prayers and Bible study, we will stumble. Accepting Christ should produce accountability and responsibility. Spiritual prayers allows us to be in visual contact with God at all times. It is never hindered by natural sight. Spiritual prayers visualize what is, not what seems to be. If you want to see Jesus throughout your day to day, pray for nothing and thank Him for everything. We are formed by who we worship and what we pray for. Jesus gave Peter the power to walk on water, but once he took his eyes off of Jesus, he saw and felt the storm surrounding him and he started to sink. Only after he refocused on Jesus and took His hand did he regain his composure and weathered the storm.

#289 *"We must find scriptural ways to bring sense and meaning to our daily lives."*

We know that the Bible makes spiritual sense out of temporal circumstances and it is our responsibility to know Jesus in the moment; we have no excuses in regard to life in the now. Our confession will train our minds and the overflow of our hearts should be praise and worship through it all. God's word helps us to get through not get by. Getting through the obstacle course called life means that we have not doubted Jesus spiritual cadence. We observe and we conquer, living for eternity one moment at a time. Getting by is just the opposite, it is all about survival not surrender. It is seeing obstacles and not Jesus, it is where emotional wounds take the place of God's eternal word and it is soul driven choices ruling over spiritual commonsense. Your faith will help you to get through, while your fear will force you to get by.

The one question I prefer never to hear from Jesus is, "Can you see Me now?" This means that I have neglected my responsibility to be one with Christ and to see His glory through all trials in life. What if taking on sainthood means we make a statement that reflects our faith and love for God, our commitment to accountability, our willingness to worship and give thanks; what would that statement be that would resonate throughout our being? If believing is seeing, it could not be anything less than, "I can see you now!" God is at work in us to will and to do according to His good pleasure, no matter what is going on or not happening. Jesus will cause all things to work for the good to those who love Him and are called according to His purpose. Seeing the God picture and getting through the snapshots of life will not only perfect you, but it will also set an example for others who need edifying in the sphere of life around them. Remember: It is the opposite of this world that will defeat the opposition of God. See Jesus based on what you know to be true spiritually and you will overcome the natural boundaries of this world. Do not be impatient with God, trust His plan and purpose in the Spirit where His power provides everything pertaining to life.

#23 *"Our human tendencies are to prune our godly attributes instead of letting God prune our human tendencies."*

Our human nature will always challenge our spiritual responsibilities; it sees in the natural and reacts to what it sees. But seeing is not believing. The attributes of God are supernatural, His omniscience, omnipresence and omnipotence can only be visible by faith in His word. Once we have learned to walk in the Spirit of God, we will be able to see the attributes of God at work in our day to day.

TAKING ON SAINTHOOD

Chapter Twenty
You Are Worthy Of It All

Paul refers to himself as a bond servant of Jesus Christ. He uses the Greek word doulos, which means to be bound to another, whose will is swallowed up in the will of another. The book of Philippians begins with, "Paul and Timothy, bondservants to Christ Jesus." Because Paul was bound to Jesus, he was not distracted by the natural barriers surrounding him. Chains could not imprison his heart and mind, and God's will be done for him was a lifestyle of praise and power. Our proclamation throughout our day to day should be, " You are worthy of it all; all of our praise, our focus, our thanks, our trust, our breath and will. Who we are and all we have is because of You."

#543 "The true source of what irritates us is not our external circumstances, but the resistance of our wills to do the will of God."

The hope we have in Christ is our only absolute certainty. The world is in our hearts, we deal with the world as we allow Jesus to deal with our hearts. Are you swallowed up by the will of God? Not sometimes, not in certain places, not only when people are watching, but at all times. To be bound in Christ is to love Jesus and serve others before satisfying self. And usually by the time you get to satisfying self you are so swallowed up by the will of God that you have no desire to do so. Philippians 1:6 tells us, "For I am confident of this very thing, that He who began a good work in you will perfect it until the day of Christ Jesus."

We are destined to be perfected; God always finishes what He starts and our lives are His responsibility no matter what the circumstances are. There is only one thing that God cannot overcome through our journey and that is our free will to choose. Perfection will be established on earth when Jesus comes again. Until then we are free to choose and God is limited to those choices. God will never stop working His majesty in our lives if we let Him.

#552 *"There comes a time when God's provisions will require our obedience to trust Him."*

Enjoying the journey always comes back to faith and not sight, trust and not understanding. Our confidence must be built on knowing not seeing. The power to become must happen before the power to overcome is necessary. When we are truly persuaded that God is and nothing else matters, our waiting on the Lord is timeless and our worship is not limited by what we are going through, but instead what God has already accomplished. We must be blinded by the light in order to see Jesus in the darkness, believing is seeing. Philippians 1:9-11 says, "And this I pray, that your love may abound still more and more in real knowledge and all discernment, so that you may approve the things that are excellent, in order to be sincere and blameless until the day of Christ; having been filled with the fruit of righteousness which comes through Jesus Christ, to the glory and praise of God." He is worthy of it all. God has given us His word to develop trust in His character. Faith comes by hearing and hearing the word of God. Paul's prayer for us is that our love will exceed the ordinary and go beyond the necessary, farther and longer than anyone's expectations. However, this only comes through true knowledge and all discernment. This knowledge is found in a personal relationship with Jesus, experiencing the power of love and producing an eternal perspective which provides you with the ability to discern right from wrong. Walking in the Spirit of God becomes your reality in spite of the world around you. This love, knowledge and discernment allows us to approve the things that are excellent. When you settle for second-best in your life you ignore God's best for your life.

#713 *"Faith focuses beyond the moment and embraces the eternal purpose of God in the moment."*

Embrace excellence in your journey and you will find a light at the end of every tunnel, a clear conscience void of doubt and blame in the moment. If your knowledge is not eternal, you will make choices based on the temporal once again falling into a soul driven lifestyle where emotions rule and self-satisfaction becomes your goal in life. If you are filled with the fruit of righteousness through Christ Jesus, praise and glory will be your supernatural response to the Father in every occasion. Praise acknowledges His glory. His presence does not have to be seen in order for Him to be visible; that is what faith in the moment is all about. Your peace and contentment will reflect salvation to the sphere of life around you and will defeat the schemes of your enemies. Do not allow privilege and prejudice to hinder God's love and your trust. Jesus set aside the privilege of God and humbled Himself taking on the form of man. He emptied Himself, not seeing equality with God something to be grasped. The sacrifice of Jesus started before He was crucified on earth. A decision was made in heaven long before Jesus took His first breath in this world. It is hard to imagine this kind of love and commitment; it is truly unbelievable, it is a challenge to our belief system. Once we accept the reality that God is unbelievable, we will be able to have faith in the God that makes no sense in this world, yet provides spiritual sense in our world. Jesus said if you have seen Me, you have seen the Father. To know Jesus is to see God. How can God give me peace in conflict? I do not know how but He does; He is unbelievable. His love casts out fear. I do not know how but He does; He is unbelievable. He causes all things to work for the good to those who love Him and are called according to His purpose.

I do not know how but He does; He is unbelievable.

Until we accept the fact that God is far beyond our vain imagination and He is truly unbelievable, will we take part in the spiritual fruit of faith, for He is worthy of it all. In Christ, hope is our spiritual imagination.

> #749 *"When we lose hope we begin to make choices based on our feelings in the moment instead of waiting on God's plan for eternity."*

In other words, hope takes the place of our imagination. Before Jesus, we imagined based on our limited perspective of life, now that we are in Christ, we have a joyful anticipation of God at work in us and for us. Philippians 2:12:13 says, "...work out your salvation with fear and trembling; for it is God who is at work in you, both to will and to work for His good pleasure." Paul is not telling us to work for salvation but work out our salvation. The Greek word for work here means 'to work to the end point'. Count the cost before you imagine the worst and in that moment rejoice in God's unbelievable plan and purpose for your life. Joy is a true reflection of trust in Jesus. When we are easily overwhelmed with our circumstances, we become the center of our problems. It is better to be first to rejoice than quick to repent. If we choose not to believe, disobedience is but a short distance away. You do not have to know all the answers in life to draw a godly conclusion that results in victory; keep your feet on the ground and your head and heart in the clouds. Hope is the uplifting attribute of God that causes all hell to break loose and Jesus identified as the way truth and life at any given moment in time.

#759 *"God can rescue us at any time and if He doesn't, He has a better plan beyond our understanding."*

Determine in your heart to know nothing except Jesus Christ, crucified for the glory of God, (1 Corinthians 2:2) and then teach your mind to hold every thought captive in obedience to Christ. This resolution will help you to rejoice in your trials and give you ears to hear and eyes to see God at work even if it does not look that way. Faith is believing God is in control of how and why we get to go through what we go through. Until we accept this reality we will live life on an emotional edge instead of a solid foundation.

Before the ascension of Jesus in Acts 1, He tells His disciples to stay in Jerusalem until the Holy Spirit comes to them not many days from now. Acts 1:6-8 shares this account, "So when they had come together, they were asking Him, saying, 'Lord is it at this time You are restoring the kingdom of Israel?' He said to them, 'It is not for you to know times or epochs which the Father has fixed by His own authority; but you will receive power when the Holy Spirit has come upon you; and you shall be My witnesses both in Jerusalem, and in all Judea and Samaria, and even to the remotest part of the earth'." His disciples are asking Him if physical change will take place when the Holy Spirit comes. We find ourselves asking the same questions, will my health be restored, will the Holy Spirit heal my loneliness, depression, fear, finances and broken relationships? The Father has fixed a time for every season under heaven, He has given us the Holy Spirit to empower us to be witnesses of His faithfulness through each season. God's plan is always better than our presumption.

#663 *"Trusting Jesus never needs a reason; it's foundation is God's love and that is always enough to rejoice and endure the path set before us."*

The Lordship of Jesus is not threatened by the seasons of our lives. If worshiping Jesus is not the air we breathe, trials will suffocate us. Trust involves knowing; I trust the chair I am sitting in right now and I know it is not going anywhere. Sadly at times, we trust chairs more than the Lordship of Jesus. Jeremiah 17:7 says, "Blessed is the man who trusts in the Lord, and whose trust is the Lord." God's love in Christ is all the trust we need to make seasons in our lives purposeful. Jesus is the reason for the season, not just Christmas but in every change in life that comes our way. The power to endure through the Holy Spirit is centered on the Lordship of Jesus. It is honorable to receive Jesus as your savior and repent of your sins, but it is godly to submit to Jesus as Lord and surrender to His will. Jeremiah is saying that trust should never involve circumstances, only our relationship with Jesus. The uncertainty of circumstances is not the foundation of God's love; Jesus is. So why waste time being intoxicated with the seasons in life when you can stand fast in the liberty wherefore Christ has set you free and not be entangled again with the yoke of bondage. Let this be our prayer each day, "Lord I know that nothing will happen today that you and I together cannot handle."

#803 *"Our spiritual point of view needs to outlast our temporal circumstances."*

We can see things as they are or believe God for what is to be. The Holy Spirit is our spiritual guide and the Bible is our road map through temporal circumstances. Spiritual stamina is key in overcoming carnal curiosity; we cannot give in to vain imagination or anything that raises itself above our knowledge of God. You do not debate with doubt, only rebuke it. I know that some trials in life may seem insurmountable, but remember, we serve an unbelievable God whose power is not seen with the natural eye but through spiritual discernment. Yes miracles happen, praise God for them, but if you are waiting to see God's miracles instead of being one you are missing the point. Jesus referred to His cousin John as a great man, no one was greater than John. Yet there are no recorded miracles in the Bible in regard to John the Baptist, unless you want to count his presence at the baptism of Jesus when the heavens opened, the Holy Spirit came down upon Jesus and the Father spoke.

Let our praise in the midst of the storm always be, "You are worthy of it all." Our lives are to reflect the results of what God's power can accomplish on the dark side of earth.

TAKING ON SAINTHOOD

Chapter Twenty One

Stand Guard

I am amazed at how often I find myself learning godly principles yet failing to apply them in my life. Knowledge is the accumulation of facts; wisdom is the application of knowledge. 1 Timothy 6:20–21 tells us, "O Timothy, guard what has been entrusted to you, avoiding worldly and empty chatter and the opposing arguments of what is falsely called 'knowledge'-which some have professed and thus gone astray from the faith. Grace be with you." Paul tells Timothy the world is filled with knowledge but without godly wisdom it is no more than empty chatter, clanging symbols in the marketplace, noise with no divine direction. Without faithful application, change will be spoken of but never achieved. Knowledge in itself can be dangerous but knowledge that experiences God through faith produces wise choices. Experiential knowledge is what has been given to us and this knowledge must be guarded and protected in our thoughts, words and deeds. If our study does not produce change then our teaching will produce hypocrisy. When we guard what has been entrusted to us, we will overcome the temptation to entertain opposing arguments that are nothing more than empty chatter in the light of scriptural truth.

#1068 *"Maturity is reflected in the time it takes to respond to God's purpose for life after reacting to the very thing that fulfills God's purpose in life."*

I Timothy 6:12 says "Fight the good fight of faith; take hold of the eternal life to which you were called, and you made the good confession in the presence of many witnesses." Standing guard is a battle that takes faith beyond your belief system and into your day to day behavior. It is that part of you that must stand firm when righteous indignation tries to take control and justification for anger pleads its case. Let us be clear, righteous indignation is sin and anger does not achieve the righteousness of God. We have been entrusted with God's love, mercy and grace. When we guard what has been entrusted to us, the one constant should be holiness. Life may not seem fair at times, but our faith in Jesus produces holy ground and in the midst of worldly chatter and opposing arguments, we stand for truth and display godly wisdom. It takes a pure heart, disciplined mind and willing soul to stand guard for the love of Jesus.

#207 *"Don't give others what they deserve, give them what God gives you."*

Our love for Jesus will reflect to a lost world, but more important to the sphere of life around us, that Jesus is real and that He is the only way to see eternal life in the now. For when we lose our eternal perspective we need not look any further than God's love being set aside to embrace righteous indignation.

When Paul admonishes Timothy to guard what was entrusted to him, he concludes with "grace be with you." This phrase was not just thrown in as an afterthought. It literally adjusts Timothy's perspective by reminding him that all that was given to him from God was unmerited. What God has entrusted to him should never be tainted with a worldview, but instead giving to others what God has given him. Ephesians 2:8-9 says, "For by grace you have been saved through faith; and that not of yourselves, it is the gift of God; not as a result of works, so that no one may boast." God's love, mercy and grace are the foundation blocks of His redemption plan. Ephesians 2:4-5 tells us, "But God, being rich in mercy, because of His great love with which He loved us, even when we were dead in our transgressions, made us alive together with Christ."

#1152 *"Discipline is following through with a commitment long after the emotion of making that commitment has passed."*

Fear and fairness are instruments in the devil's attack against what has been entrusted to us. Fairness debates God's timing and purpose in our lives. When we entertain fairness it usually means we want God to change His plan and bring justice to our circumstances. And if justice is not attained, the spirit of fear will dictate an emotional reaction. Sometimes our greatest fear is that God is not giving others what they deserve. There lies mercy and grace initiated by God's unconditional love, the very same character qualities of God that He has shown towards us. II Timothy 1:7 tells us, "For God has not given to us a spirit of timidity, but of power and love and discipline." We have no problem being gifted with power and love, but discipline seems like an odd gift from God. Yet without discipline our thoughts will be renegade, our words inappropriate and our actions ungodly. Godly discipline has everything to do with our spirit and communion with God and should not be enhanced with our feelings. Discipline comes from the word disciple which in the Greek means learner. Simply said, when we are disciplined we are committed to what we learn spiritually. God's love has given us the power to follow through with our commitments. Prior to verse 7, Paul actually tells Timothy to kindle afresh the gift of God within him. We should not limit this to the gifts of the Spirit or the foundational gifts of redemption, mercy and grace. The fruit of the Spirit is a gift from God; His power, His plan, His purpose are gifts from God. There is no end to God's gifting, making our kindling afresh God's gift to us a never-ending worship service.

#1149 *"Worship should not be a part of repentance but a song of deliverance."*

A disciplined mind eliminates divisive thoughts and is not interested if God does not receive the glory. Our background music in life should always be songs of deliverance, that is a lifestyle of worship. Praying for nothing and worshiping in everything is key to standing guard over God's gift. Psalms 32:7–8 says, "You are my hiding place; You preserve me from trouble; You surround me with songs of deliverance. Selah. I will instruct you and teach you in the way which you should go; I will counsel you with My eye upon you." This is a Psalm of David in which he speaks and God answers him.

The book of Psalms are songs of deliverance that preserve us. As we sing songs of deliverance we ourselves create our own book of Psalms unto God. And His response will be the same as to David, 'I will instruct you and teach you in the way which you should go; I will counsel you with My eye upon you.' So when we find ourselves learning godly principles but failing to apply them in our lives, quickly begin to sing those songs of deliverance. Worship may start off as part of repentance but as we train ourselves to stand guard over what has been entrusted to us and avoid worldly chatter and opposing arguments, our worship will be always and not only in times of crisis. The Spirit of wisdom will rule our hearts and disciple our souls to glorify Jesus through it all.

#701 *"Trials are necessary, but it's not necessary that we become less loving and less powerful because of them."*

Do not view standing guard as a defensive position. View it as a watchmen posted on the walls of your spiritual temple, seeing the trials in life as teachable moments for you and the sphere of life around you. Trials are important steps in the right direction. When we guard our gift defensively we are reacting to life instead of responding to God. This reaction takes our eyes off of Jesus and onto the trials. We will either stand guard with the sword of the Spirit or fall prey to the schemes of the enemy, remember your adversary the devil is prowling around like a roaring lion looking for someone to devour, but you must resist him firm in your faith. (1 Peter 5:8-9) A sure sign of warring defensively is discontentment in which our soul takes point and we begin to make decisions based on our feelings. The gift of power and love fades with every emotional outburst and we quickly lose joy and the song of deliverance. Worship sounds the alarm that God is faithful and trials are necessary.

Standing guard is what constant Christianity is all about. Revelation 12:10 says that satan accuses the brethren day and night. If that be the case then rejoicing always, praying without ceasing and in everything giving thanks makes complete and necessary sense.

#504 "Submit to the word of God, obey the will of God and accept the ways of God."

The devil left Jesus in the wilderness looking for a more opportune time. (Luke 4:13) His constant accusations towards us and others are for the purpose of wearing us down. John 10:10 says, "The thief comes only to steal and kill and destroy; I came that they may have life, and have it abundantly." We must resist him firm in our faith; spiritual stamina is vital for success in the now. Just as the devil will never stop accusing us we must never stop worshiping God. I am convinced that we should not live on yesterday's victories, but find ways to be vigilant in our spiritual walk every day. One area of Christianity that will help keep us focused is communion. Jesus set this time aside for us to remember His great sacrifice leading to our redemption. However, we have turned it into a religious sacrament instead of a time of sanctification.

Communion is so much more than eating crackers and juice on Sunday morning, as significant as that may be. It was His last meal with His disciples prior to His crucifixion. Broken bread in memory of a broken body and wine signifying His shed blood. Think of the impact communion would have in our day to day if we treated the consumption of food and drink as our last supper in remembrance of God's redeeming us through Jesus Christ our Savior? First of all our communion would not be weekly but 3, 4, 5, times a day. The time we would spend in communion would bring attention to the need for more of God's love, mercy and grace to flow in and through our lives. The principles we learn would be easily applied because of the constant reminder communion would place in our lives. I Peter 3:15-17 says, "but sanctify Christ as Lord in your hearts, always being ready to make a defense to everyone who asks you to give an account for the hope that is in you, yet with gentleness and reverence; and keep a good conscience so that in the thing in which you are slandered, those who revile your good behavior in Christ will be put to shame. For it is better, if God should will it so, that you suffer for doing what is right rather than for doing what is wrong." Communion as a lifestyle sets Jesus apart in our hearts, and keeps us ready to defend the hope that is in us with gentleness and reverence, keeping a clear conscience in all that we say and do.

#856 *"Praying without ceasing is a sure sign of faith in God's presence."*

Standing guard with an attitude of prayer is key to successful living. Always looking to Jesus for advice and comfort, direction and peace, will help keep us from being distracted by the trials in life. We will find ourselves standing on holy ground whenever we acknowledge the name of Jesus in the midst of trying times. Praying in the Spirit reinforces us and places eternity back in the now. We can be victorious today because we have hope for tomorrow. Joy should spring up when Jesus is acknowledged and our conversation with

God becomes holy communion, confirming that our God reigns over every detail of our lives. II Timothy 1:13-14 says, "Retain the standard of sound words which you have heard from me, in the faith and love which are in Christ Jesus. Guard, through the Holy Spirit who dwells in us, the treasure which has been entrusted to you." Paul encourages Timothy to hold the pattern of his teaching through faith and love in Christ. Echo that which you have been taught, repeat the example of truth over and over again in faith and love. Faith being the assurance of things hoped for and the conviction of things not seen, causing us to see Jesus, knowing that His love removes fear, covers a multitude of sins and never fails. Stand guard through the Holy Spirit, over the treasure that has been entrusted to you. Guard what has been given to you by God, treasure it, value it above and beyond anything that this world can provide. Make it your own, protect with diligence what God has gifted you in Christ.

#1163 *"We can see things as they are or believe God for what is to be."*

Jesus tells us to store up for ourselves treasure in heaven where neither moth nor rust destroys, and where thieves do not break in or steal; for where your treasure is, there your heart will be also. (Matthew 6:20–21) Our treasure exposes our heart, the choices we make reflect what we value most. If we do not stand guard over the blessings of God and treasure them, we will succumb to temporal circumstances that distract us from our eternal purpose. When we treasure the love of Jesus, our choices will glorify God. Taking on sainthood is standing guard in the liberty wherefore Christ has set us free and not being entangled with the yoke of bondage. Faith working through love should be our motto in a world filled with empty chatter and opposing views. When our choices are debatable we are slipping away from the known will of God in Christ.

#716 "The kingdom of God is not a place but a lifestyle."

Taking on sainthood is living in the kingdom where the gifts of God become our lifestyle. Everything pertaining to Jesus and scripture should flow supernaturally throughout our lives. We will truly enjoy the journey that God has set before us when we do not have to find a place where faith, love and hope are, but instead, be that place. Galatians 2:20 says, "I have been crucified with Christ; and it is no longer I who live, but Christ lives in me; and the life which I now live in the flesh I live by faith in the Son of God, who loved me and gave Himself up for me." We are not one with Christ if we are double minded, unstable and easily deceived. We stand guard not for what is taking place around us or to us, but within us. It is impossible to live for Jesus if we have not been crucified with Him. Dead people do not worry, they do not act unbecomingly, they do not regret words spoken or hurt feelings. Dead people have nothing and it is in that nothingness that Jesus begins His work in us. Teaching us how to live as a child of God, giving us fruit to become spiritual in a carnal world. Developing in our hearts and minds the capacity to know the truth that will set and keep us free, creating faith and love in a lost world where we must grow and they must know. The kingdom of God is in our hearts where Jesus is on the throne. It is not in a building or country as it was in times past. God's kingdom is you and me empowered by the Holy Spirit to live holy and to glorify the Father. That is what we stand guard over, the purity of the gospel message where the love of God is the only justice necessary; where our resurrected lives reflect Jesus and not the sins Jesus died for.

Made in the USA
Las Vegas, NV
24 February 2023